D0353879

Rural Life in Wessex

Rural Life in Wessex
1500–1900

J. H. Bettey

ALAN SUTTON
1987

ALAN SUTTON PUBLISHING
BRUNSWICK ROAD · GLOUCESTER

Copyright © J.H. Bettey 1987

First published in 1977
by Moonraker Press

This edition published 1987

ISBN 0-86299-425-X

Cover picture: Bridgeman Art Library

Printed in Great Britain by
The Guernsey Press Company Limited
Guernsey, Channel Islands

Contents

ACKNOWLEDGEMENTS
Grateful thanks are due to several persons and institutions who have helped
by supplying information or photographs: especially to the county archivists
of Dorset, Hampshire, Somerset and Wiltshire; to the county archaeological
societies of Dorset, Somerset and Wiltshire; to the Museum of English Rural
Life at the University of Reading; and to Alan Andrew, David Bromwich of
the Somerset Local History Library, Dr Robert Dunning, Michael Lansdown,
Adrian Moon and Kenneth Rogers; also to Mrs Rosemary Johnston and
Mrs Mary Scullard for their secretarial assistance.

Introduction The Background

The following chapters describe the life and work of the people who lived in the rural communities of a large part of southern England from the Tudor period until the end of the nineteenth century, that is from the end of the Middle Ages to the virtual ending of the horse era. The area to be described includes the counties of Wiltshire, Somerset and Dorset, and the modern county of Avon. This region reaches from the southern Cotswolds to the English channel, and from Salisbury Plain to Exmoor, and in order to understand the rural life of this large area and to appreciate the extent of the changes which have taken place in its society during the four centuries from 1500 to 1900, it is important to realise its diverse physical characteristics. For it was this physical environment, which might be modified by the labour of generations of farmers, but which could not be changed in its essentials, that above all else dictated the economic and social life of the rural communities. The outstanding physical character-istic of the whole region is the variety of its geology and landscape, and this diversity has always been the dominant influence in ordering men's work and shaping the nature of their societies. The widely different soils and landscapes, and the consequent variations in farming throughout the region, can be summarised roughly under four main headings.

First, and most dramatic, is the massive expanse of chalk downland which dominates much of Wiltshire, and radiates out from Salisbury Plain into Dorset and Hampshire. This was traditionally the area of sheep and corn, where the fertility of the cornlands was maintained by the close folding at night of the great sheep flocks which fed all day on the rolling chalk downlands. It was also the area of large estates, and of nucleated, compact villages, with settlements concentrated in the valleys of the clear, fast-running, chalk streams; while the higher ground, where water was seldom available, remained for the most part devoid of settlement and bare of woodland. Throughout most of the period from 1500 to 1900 the chalklands were the area where the manorial system remained most strongly entrenched, and where the communal system of agriculture, with the cooperative cultivation of the large common arable fields and the common pasturing of sheep and cattle, survived the longest.

The second main region comprises the clay vales and low-lying moorlands of north Wiltshire, the whole expanse of the central Somerset levels, and the vales of north and west Dorset. This was the region of small, enclosed, family farms and of scattered settlement, where dairy farming and stock raising predominated. In many places this part of the region was heavily wooded, particularly during the first half of the period, when the great royal forests like Blackmoor, Gillingham, Powerstock, Neroche, Selwood, Chippenham, Melksham and Braydon survived. Throughout most of this area farmers concentrated on the production of butter and cheese and on stock-rearing, while corn growing was of much less importance than it was on the chalk. But the vales also included some outstandingly fertile areas, most notably the Vale of Taunton Deane which was described in the early seventeenth century as 'the paradise of England'. The claylands also provided the raw materials and dairy farming gave the necessary time to support a vast range of different crafts and secondary employments, and this was also the area in which the cloth-making industry flourished. One part of it which should be mentioned separately is the Somerset levels, which during the early part of this period occupied almost half the county. Life for the majority of the inhabitants of this low-lying region resembled more closely that of the dwellers in the fens of eastern England than it did that of the neighbouring districts.

The third main division of the region consists of the hilly country of the Mendips and north Somerset, the hills and moorlands of west Somerset and the broken country of the district stretching along the Somerset-Dorset border from Chard and Crewkerne through Yeovil and beyond towards Frome. The higher parts of these areas consist of barren moorland, such as Exmoor, the Quantocks and the higher parts of Mendip, but the lower slopes are among the most fertile parts of the whole region, and east Somerset, for example, was notable for its mixed dairy and arable farming, as well as for cloth-making.

Finally, the region also includes the large, triangular heathland which stretches from its apex near Dorchester across eastern Dorset and on through part of Hampshire, including the isle of Purbeck, the large area around Poole harbour and the New Forest. This is the area so graphically described by Thomas Hardy in *The Return of the Native*, and which he called Egdon Heath. Much of the heathland consists of poor, acid soils—sands, gravels and clays—and considerable parts of it have always been unsuited to arable farming. During most of the period described here the poorest parts supported only water-logged, poor pasture, and grew little but furze, and sedge. A good deal of the heathland remains still in this undeveloped state, though large areas are now used for forestry.

Each part of the region supported different kinds of agriculture, each provided different kinds of raw materials and opportunities for industrial employments and crafts, and each gave rise to a different kind of rural society. The following chapters will discuss the farming and life of the people who lived in the different parts of the region and the way in which the rural communities changed and developed from the sixteenth to the nineteenth centuries.

For map of the area described see pages 20 and 21.

1, Farming during the sixteenth and seventeenth centuries

Over the whole region, farming has always been by far the most important occupation and, until very recently, the majority of people have obtained their livelihood directly from the land. But the farming of various districts has always been very different, and has developed in diverse ways; this diversity makes the agricultural history of the region especially interesting, and this chapter will consider the different sorts of farming which were to be found, mainly from about 1500 until the beginning of the eighteenth century, though the traditional agriculture continued in many places until well into the nineteenth century. The following chapter will then describe some of the main improvements and changes which occurred in the agriculture of the region, and the effect which these had on traditional farming practices.

THE CHALKLANDS

In the chalklands of Wiltshire, Dorset and Hampshire, sheep and corn have dominated the farming scene right up to the twentieth century. The production of corn, particularly of wheat and barley, has always been the main aim of farming in this part of the region, and until the advent of cheap and easily obtainable artificial fertilisers, the fertility of the thin chalkland soils could be maintained only by the folding of the vast flocks of sheep which were pastured on the chalk downlands. The sheep flocks were therefore an essential factor in the successful production of corn. The importance of corn-growing in the farming of the chalkland was emphasised by Robert Seymer of Hanford near Blandford Forum in a report on the husbandry of the chalk region which he presented to the recently-founded Royal Society in 1665. Seymer's report concentrated almost entirely upon arable farming, and he clearly regarded livestock as of secondary importance except for emphasising the importance of the sheep-fold. He reported that wheat was the most widely grown and valuable cereal crop, and that the two crops of wheat and barley between them accounted for most of the acreage of corn grown. The same emphasis is shown in the notebook of Robert Wansborough, who farmed at Shrewton in the Wiltshire chalkland during the 1630s. Wansborough was typical of farmers in that area in the over-riding concern which his notes reveal for his corn crops. His main interest was obviously in farming for profit, and it was from corn-growing that his main profit came. But only with the aid of very large sheep flocks could corn be grown successfully on the shallow chalk soils. Daniel Defoe, in his *Tour through England and Wales* made during the early years of the eighteenth century, like so many other travellers was greatly impressed by the number of sheep he saw everywhere on the chalk, and of the area between Winchester and Salisbury, for example, he wrote that 'the vast flocks of sheep, which one every where sees upon these downs, and the great number of those flocks, is a sight truly worth observation'; while of Dorchester he wrote, no doubt with some exaggeration, that 'there were 600,000 sheep fed on the downs within six miles of the town'. On a journey which he made between Shaftesbury and Salisbury, Defoe encountered a difficulty which must often have beset travellers across the great expanse of Salisbury Plain where there were neither clearly defined roads nor sign-posts. He wrote that the Plain

has neither house or town in view all the way, and the road which often lyes very broad, and branches off insensibly, might easily cause a traveller to loose his way, but there is a certain never failing assistance upon all these downs for telling a stranger his way, and that is the number of shepherds feeding, or keeping their vast flocks of sheep, which are every where in the way, and who, with a very little pains, a traveller may always speak with.

These very large sheep flocks continued to be one of the principal features of the chalkland areas up to the end of the nineteenth century.

The main object of keeping sheep was for the dung which they deposited while folded on the arable land, and although the wool, lambs and mutton produced by the sheep were a useful source of profit for farmers, these were nonetheless secondary to the main function. Edward Lisle, who farmed at Crux Easton on the Hampshire chalkland from 1693 until his death in 1722, and whose book *Observations in Husbandry* was an important farming manual of the eighteenth century, emphasised the vital connection between the sheep-fold and corn production, and wrote that '. . . if a bane fell on sheep, corn would be dear, because there could not be a fifth part of the folding that otherwise there would be, and consequently a deficiency of the crop'. This continued to be true during much of the next two centuries. In a valuation of the manor of Sydling St Nicholas in Dorset, part of the estates of Winchester college, in 1776, the surveyor commented on the sheep walks that 'The sheep are kept primarily to produce manure for the Arable Lands, which is the greatest profit gained by them'. Thomas Davis, who was steward to Lord Bath at Longleat, in a Report on the Agriculture of Wiltshire prepared for the Board of Agriculture in 1794 wrote that 'The first and principal purpose of keeping sheep is undoubtedly the dung of the sheepfold, and the second is the wool'.

For much of this period the sheep kept on the chalklands were the ancestors of what were later to become the Dorset and Wiltshire 'Horn' breeds. They were bred for their ability to walk the long distances from their downland pastures to the arable fields, and for their readiness to be close folded at night on the cornlands. They were large, active and hardy animals, with long sturdy legs, able to find their food on the steep and exposed downs. As with their modern successors, both ewes and rams had curled horns. The sheep-fold was the central feature of chalkland agriculture, and the method by which the sheep were folded was described in detail by many writers. Thomas Davis, for example, in the Report on the Agriculture of Wiltshire, described the way in which the sheep were penned every night by the shepherd into a fold made of hurdles, and how each day the fold was moved so that the whole field was eventually covered. Davis wrote that

In the common fields, sheep which are sent by the occupiers of yard-lands (i.e. the individual tenements) are kept in one flock, by a common shepherd, and folded regularly over the whole field, shifting the fold every night. The size of the fold is regulated by the size of the field they have to cover, so as to get over the whole in time for sowing: but the usual rule is, to allow one thousand sheep, to fold what they call a tenantry acre (about three fourths of a statute acre) per night.

In a similar Report on the Agriculture of Dorset in 1793 John Claridge also emphasised the importance of the sheep-fold. He stated that

The sheep are constantly attended by a shepherd the whole day, whose wages is six shillings per week, a great coat yearly, and a breakfast on a Sunday. A dog is found and maintained by the shepherd, and the master has the skins of the dead sheep. . . . The wether sheep are constantly folded all the year round, running over the ewe leas or downs by day, and are penned on the tillage by night; they are penned late in the evening, and let out from the fold before sunrise in the winter, and not later than six o'clock in the summer. . . . in general the size of the hurdle is about four feet six inches long, three feet six inches high, made chiefly of hazle, with ten upright sticks; and fifteen dozen of them, with a like number of stakes and wriths, to confine them together, will inclose a statute acre of ground, and will contain twelve or thirteen hundred sheep therein very commodiously. The hurdles are moved every morning, consequently the same number of sheep will manure an acre of land daily.

For an efficient sheep-fold it was essential to have a large number of sheep, so that on most chalkland manors the sheep of all the tenants were kept in a single, common flock with a shepherd who was employed by the whole manor. The regulations for the conduct of the shepherd on the Wiltshire chalkland manor of Heale near Salisbury, which were drawn up in 1629 by the tenants meeting in the manorial court, set out precisely both the duties of the shepherd and the obligations of the tenants. These are typical of many similar agreements for other chalkland manors. The shepherd was to 'diligently attend and keepe his flocke' at all times, and was not to leave the task to deputies or to children. He was to see that the sheep did not stray, and that they did no damage to the growing corn. He was to inform the owner at once if any sheep was sick or if it died; and 'if any sheepe be killed with stones or dogges or otherwise through the defaulte of ye Shepherd the Shepherd shall pay the owner for the same as two Tenants shall value it, otherwise to be deducted out of his wages.' The shepherd had to move the fold each day and pen the sheep in the fold each evening. He was also to 'keepe his sheepe from the scabb or other breakinge out as much as possibly he may, and forthwith treat and cure them yf any happen to be scabby.' Finally he was to see that only those who had the right to do so brought sheep to his flock, and that they did not exceed their proper number. The tenants for their part were to contribute to the shepherd's wages in proportion to the number of their sheep, and they were each to provide every year a stipulated number of hurdles for the fold, and an agreed quantity of hay, which was to be left in the care of the shepherd for feeding to the whole flock during the winter. The tenants were also forbidden from keeping any sheep on the common lands of the manor apart from those in the care of the shepherd. Any tenant who failed to keep his part of the agreement would lose the benefit of the common fold on his arable land. This last point was not an idle threat, for at Heale shortly after the agreement was made it was ordered by the manorial court that 'Robert Atkins in regard of his insolencye to the Lord of this Mannor nowe in open Courte, and for refuzinge to obey the orders of this Courte, shall not from henceforthe have the benefytt of the flocke to come upon his Lande.'

The need for a common sheep flock to manure the ground was one of the main reasons why the communal organisation of agriculture survived longest on the chalklands. The compact villages and the shape of the chalkland manors, long and narrow, stretching from the river valley often for two or three miles up on to the high downland, also helped to preserve the power of the manorial court and made the communal organisation of agriculture at once much easier and much more important than it was in the scattered farmsteads and broken countryside of the clayland areas. In the chalklands the common arable fields survived, often until they were enclosed by an Act of Parliament in the nineteenth century, and the tenants continued to hold their land in strips or parcels scattered over the two or three large open fields of the manor. The chalkland manors often also had their cattle in a common herd under the care of a cowherd who, like the shepherd, was employed by the whole manor. For example, at Affpuddle in Dorset in 1600 it was agreed by the tenants meeting in the manorial court that

Nicholas White shall from hensforthe be the common herdman for governynge and guidinge of the Tenants Cattle of Affpudle. And that he shal be payed by the owners of the Cattle, the first yere a Cloake, and everie twoe yeares after a Cloake and for every day 1d. And have her or his deputies meate and drinke att everie of theire houses in order, one after another.

Many other chalkland manors had similar arrangements which continued throughout the seventeenth and eighteenth centuries. The cowherd received the cattle each morning after the morning milking and returned them to their owners each evening, and the customs of many manors forbade the tenants from grazing their cattle in the common pasture unless they were in the charge of the cowherd. Under the cowherd's control the common grazing would be carefully managed and eaten by the cattle in a prescribed order. The regulations which survive for several manors setting out the regular course in which different parts of the commons, fallows and stubbles were to be grazed in turn are an impressive denial of the idea of uncontrolled grazing which is sometimes alleged as a failing of the system of common field agriculture. A more justifiable cause of criticism is the fact that selective breeding and improvement of livestock was very difficult, if not impossible, because on many manors there was a common bull and a common boar. Often it was the responsibility of the lord of the manor or his representative or of the parson to provide a suitable bull and boar. For example the customs of the manor Piddlehinton in Dorset, belonging to Eton College, were set out in detail in 1571, and these included the provision of a bull and a boar by whoever had taken the lease of the demesne lands of the manor; likewise the parson at Poyntington, on the borders of Somerset and Dorset, was to provide a bull for the tenants' cows, and 'for everie sowe which anie of the Inhabitantes shall keepe to breed pigges, the parson is to keepe a sufficient bore to increase the same at his own Chardge.' The manor of Winterborne Monkton, in the shadow of the great hill-fort of Maiden Castle, had an unusual variation on these customs, for it was stated there in 1733 that

the Churchwardens and Overseers of the Poor of this parish shall in every year find and provide an able Bull for the use of the Dairy Cows of this mannor, and if the Bull follows any bullard cow into any of the Tenants backsides he shall not be driven out or molested till his business is done . . . .

As we have said, the main crops of the chalkland were wheat and barley, and some farmers also grew occasional crops of rye and oats or of peas and beans. Changes that occurred during this period, which will be considered in detail in the next chapter, consisted mainly of the introduction of fodder crops such as vetches, turnips, clover and rape into the crop rotation of the common fields. Before the introduction of improved agricultural methods during the eighteenth and nineteenth centuries, regular fallowing every second or third year was considered essential on the light chalk soils, even with the advantage of the sheep-fold, if they were to bear satisfactory crops. The regular course of cropping was to grow wheat after the fallow. The land was left during the summer fallow, with occasional stirring to kill the weeds, and during this period it had the benefit of any dung that was available, as well as of the sheep. The wheat was sown broadcast, often as early as mid-September. Barley followed the wheat crop, the ground having been ploughed after harvest, and having the benefit both of frost and of the sheepfold during the winter; the barley was then sown in the spring. It was a major disadvantage of the system of common field agriculture that tenants could not easily or conveniently grow crops which demanded a different timetable from those grown by the majority, for as soon as a crop was harvested the fields were thrown open to sheep and cattle for grazing. Vetches or other fodder crops were occasionally grown in the common fields, but these had to be fenced to secure them from damage when the fields were thrown open. It was this inconvenience which was the main cause of the extinction of the system, and of its replacement by enclosures.

THE CLAYLANDS

In the clayland areas of north Wiltshire, north and west Dorset and parts of Somerset, and in the very extensive areas of marshland and fens in Somerset as well as in the hilly country of the Mendips, the Quantocks,

Exmoor and the Somerset-Dorset border, the pattern of farming throughout the whole of the period from 1500 to 1900 was quite different from that of the chalklands. Much of the clay area had already been enclosed into small family farms before 1500, or was enclosed by piecemeal agreements between tenants during the sixteenth and seventeenth centuries. Although there were many compact, nucleated villages—some of them quite large—settlement was not by any means confined to these villages and a great many of the people lived in scattered and isolated farmsteads and hamlets; and although in some places the common arable fields did survive in the claylands, these were far less usual than on the chalk. The main aim of most clayland farming was the production of milk to be turned into butter and cheese, and the rearing of cattle and pigs. Some cattle were also brought into the region for fattening, many of them coming from Wales. Arable farming was far less important, and although some farmers grew corn for their own use and to provide winter feed for their livestock, there were many 'all-grass' farms with little or no arable land. Sheep played a much less crucial role in the farming of these areas, though some farmers on the higher ground bred sheep for sale to chalkland farmers or in order to produce fat sheep and lambs for the market. Manorial control was far less strong and rigid in the clayland areas since there was much less communal organisation of agriculture.

In Wiltshire the chalk and the clay or cheese country are perhaps more clearly divided one from another than anywhere else in the region, and the distinction has given rise to the saying 'as different as chalk from cheese'. John Aubrey, the Wiltshire historian and antiquarian of the seventeenth century, drew a very clear contrast between the two parts of the county when he wrote of the clay vales of north Wiltshire that

hereabout is but little tillage or hard labour, they only milk the cowes and make cheese; they feed chiefly on milke meates, which cooles their braines too much, and hurts their inventions. These circumstances make them melancholy, contemplative, and malicious; by consequence whereof come more law suites out of North Wilts, at least double to the Southern parts. And by the same reason they are generally more apt to be fanatiques . . . .

Whereas of the Wiltshire chalkland he wrote:

On the downs sc. the south part, where 'tis all upon tillage, and where the shepherds labour hard, their flesh is hard, their bodies strong; being weary after hard labour, they have not leisure to read and contemplate of religion, but goe to bed to their rest, to rise betime the next morning to their labour.

Although cattle formed the back-bone of clayland farming, it was not until the nineteenth century that there was much specialisation in the breeds or varieties which were kept. It is probable that the red Devon cattle predominated in the western part of the region, while the Longhorn and Old Gloucester breeds were more common in Wiltshire, but there is little definite evidence about this, and there was certainly a great deal of movement of cattle and inter-mixing of varieties, while many black cattle from Wales were also brought into the region for fattening before being driven on to market in London and other towns. The result was that most districts had a mixture of types, and few farmers confined themselves to any one particular variety. John Aubrey, writing of north Wiltshire in the seventeenth century, said that all types and colours of cattle were to be found there, and that most were a mixture of colours: 'The country hereabout is much inclined to pied cattle, but commonly the colour is black, or brown, or deep red.'

As late as 1812 William Stevenson could write of Dorset that:

There is no select breed of cattle in this county; the dairy cows of the chalky district, and the south-eastern parts of the county, are a long horned kind, rather short in the leg, with white backs and bellies, and dark spotted or brindled sides. They are a mixture of various breeds from Hampshire and other neighbouring counties, and more regard is paid to the quantity of milk they are likely to produce, than to any other quality. . . . In the western part of the county as well as in the vale of Blackmoor, the cows are mostly of the Devonshire kind.

During much of the period from 1500 to 1900 it was a widespread practice throughout large parts of Somerset, Wiltshire and Dorset for farmers to rent out their dairy cows to a dairyman by the year. Under this system the farmer provided the cows, together with the necessary pasture and winter fodder, as well as a house for the dairyman and a dairy in return for an annual rent per cow, while the dairyman made his profit from the sale of milk, butter and cheese. A description of such a rented dairy in the Frome valley in Dorset is the fictional account given by Thomas Hardy in *Tess of the d'Urbervilles* of the large dairy rented by dairyman Richard Crick. There seems to be no single over-riding reason why the practice of renting dairies became such a popular feature of the agricultural life of the region, and it is likely that several factors contributed. The concentration of the larger farmers upon corn and sheep and their reluctance to become in-involved in the day-to-day management of a dairy, the labour-intensive and specialist nature of dairy work, the problems which were inevitable in the manufacture and storage of butter and cheese and in the marketing of these products, may all have led farmers to rent out their cows. For many men in the region who lacked sufficient capital or the opportunity to start up in farming themselves, but who, with their families, were prepared to work the long hours every day demanded by milking cows and dairy work, renting a small herd of cows was an important first step on the road to becoming a farmer. The practice of renting out cows was roundly condemned by many of the agricultural 'improvers' of the eighteenth and nineteenth centuries. For example William Marshall complained that the system deterred both farmer and dairyman from making any improvements in either breeds of cows or in methods; and Arthur Young wholeheartedly condemned the whole idea on similar grounds and, with typical scorn, asked, 'Was ever there such a ridiculous system known?' In spite of these and many other critics, however, the practice continued to be common in the region throughout the nineteenth century.

Much of the milk produced in the regions was used for the production of cheese, and a variety of different kinds were made. In north Wiltshire a full-milk cheese was made, known variously as 'Gloucester' cheese from its resemblance to the cheese of the nearby vale of Berkeley, or as 'Marlborough' or 'North Wilts'. In Dorset, where large quantities of butter were also produced, several skim-milk cheeses were made, among them the famous 'Blue Vinny' or 'Vinney' cheese. The cheese of the Somerset levels was destined to become the best-known of all cheeses, the Cheddar. Defoe described in some detail the co-operative effort by which this cheese was made in Cheddar itself during the early eighteenth century.

The milk of all the town cows, is brought together every day into a common room, where the persons appointed, or trusted for the management, measure every man's quantity, and set it down in a book; when the quantities are adjusted, the milk is all put together, and every meal's milk makes one cheese, and no more; so the cheese is bigger, or less as the cows yield more, or less, milk. By this method, the goodness of the cheese is preserved, and, without all dispute, it is the best cheese that England affords if not, that the whole world affords.

As the cheeses are, by this means, very large, for they often weigh a hundred weight, sometimes much more, so the poorer inhabitants, who have but few cows, are obliged to stay the longer for the return of their milk; for no man has any such return, 'till his share comes to a whole cheese, and then he has it; and if the quantity of his milk delivered in, comes to above a cheese, the overplus rests in account to his credit, 'till another cheese comes to his share; and thus every man has equal justice, and though he should have but one cow, he shall, in time have one whole cheese. This cheese is often sold for six pence to eight pence per pound, when Cheshire cheese is sold but for two pence halfpenny.

Some butter and cheese was exported by sea, particularly from the Dorset ports and from Bristol, but most was sold through the many west-country markets and fairs, and was bought by factors for dispatch to various towns and especially to London. The markets at Marlborough, Tetbury, Wincanton, Frome and Yeovil were all famous for butter and cheese. Thomas Gerard who lived at Trent, between Sherborne and Yeovil, wrote in 1630 of the busy trade conducted in the market at Yeovil, and concluded that '. . . its greatest commodity is Cheese'; and John Aubrey later in the seventeenth century described Marlborough market as 'one of the greatest markets for cheese in the west of England. Here doe reside factors for the cheesemongers of London'. Most of the sheep and cattle which were fattened in the region were also driven to London and other towns for slaughter. The dealers and drovers who engaged in this trade were not generally the sort of people who kept records of their transactions, and details of marketing and droving are therefore rare, but the occasional references which do survive leave no doubt of the importance of this trade in the economic life of the region. Droving and all other aspects of the marketing of agricultural products will be discussed in detail in Chapter 5.

THE HEATHLAND

The agriculture of the sandy heathland of south-east Dorset and of the New Forest district of Hampshire differed markedly from that of either the chalklands or the clay. Much of the area consisted of poor, acid soils which were, and still remain, unsuited to arable farming, and most farmers therefore concentrated on the breeding of cattle, horses and pigs. In a few parts where the soil was more favourable, especially in Hampshire, rye and oats as well as some wheat could be grown, and around Corfe Castle in Dorset many farmers grew small plots of hemp. Most heathland farmers derived a considerable part of their income from other employments— quarrying, turf, peat and furze cutting, digging clay, etc.—and these by-employments will be considered in Chapter 3. Much of the land remains unenclosed, and William Stevenson's description of the area in 1812 still holds true today:

The heath land is almost entirely unenclosed, except the parts occupied by fir plantations which are surrounded by sod banks, with furze sown on top of them; and this is perhaps the best kind of fence that can be afforded for enclosures on a soil so exceedingly barren and unimprovable.

The twentieth century has seen a great increase in the area of the heathland taken up by the fir plantations of the Forestry Commission, as well as in the areas used for army training and for the extraction of clay and gravel. During the period 1500–1900 most of the animals kept on the heath were

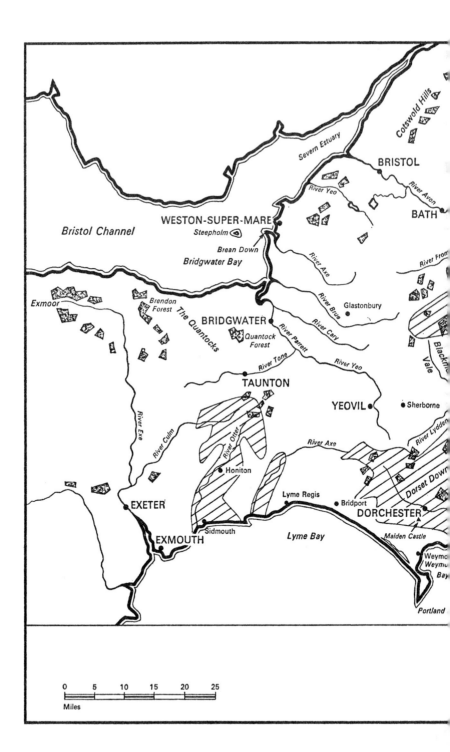

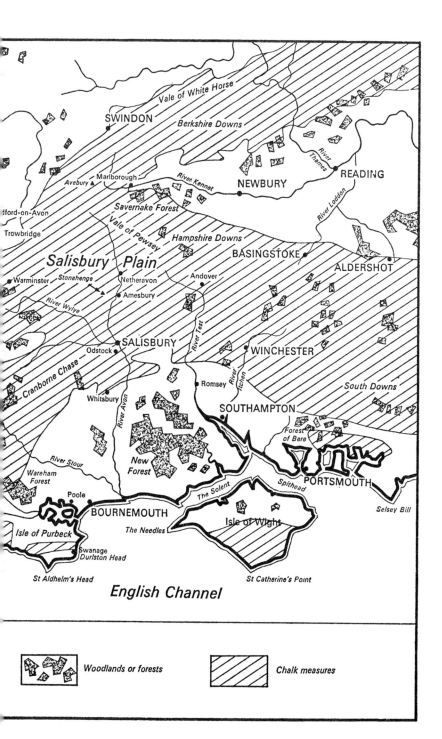

Woodlands or forests

Chalk measures

poor, undersized creatures, like the poor-quality cattle or the ponies, the 'heath-croppers', which picked up what sustenance they could from the ling and heather. An account of the agriculture of Hampshire written by Abraham and William Driver in 1794 described the horses of the New Forest area and noted that

A great number of small horses are bred upon the forests, where but little attention is paid to their shape or size, as they run promiscuously together; and from the barrenness of the soil, for want of cultivation, they are extremely small, having scarcely any thing to feed on but heath, from which they have very properly derived the appellation of *heath croppers.*

Pigs were also a speciality of some farmers in the New Forest district of Hampshire, and were fattened on the pannage of the forests. Thomas Fuller, in the seventeenth century described the way in which pigs were fattened in the Hampshire woodlands: '. . . they feed in the forest on plenty of acorns . . . which, going out lean, return home fat, without care or cost to their owners.' Pigs continued to be a very important feature of the Hampshire heathland and forest district, and the county was famous for the pork, bacon and other products of its pigs. A report on Hampshire farming prepared for the Board of Agriculture by Charles Vancouver in 1813 described the Hampshire hog as

a coarse, raw-boned, flat-sided animal, agreeing in no respect with the idea entertained of it in other parts of the Kingdom; the great number fed for a few weeks in the close of autumn, upon the mast which the forest and other woodlands produce, the county, and the excellent mode of curing hog-meat practised by the house-keepers, have contributed in a far greater degree to establish that superiority ascribed to Hampshire bacon, than any inherent excellence in its native breed of hogs.

Vancouver also included in this report a sketch of a typical small farmer on the heath and forest land, a picture which would have been as true for the Dorset heathland farmer as it was for Hampshire. This was the sort of person who was so perceptively described by Thomas Hardy in *The Return of the Native*, a novel which is dominated by the peculiar character of the heath. Vancouver's description was of a forest dweller, who

from time to time, has encroached a few perches from the forest, and which at length amounting to two or three acres, constitutes what he conceives a sort of independence to himself and family. Upon this he pretends to grow as much grass and hay as will suffice to bait his working horse, or horses, night and morning; a few potatoes; and some bread-corn for his family. His principal exertions are directed to the cutting, rearing, and carting of peat-fuel, and of procuring or removing any other combustible matter to the neighbouring towns and villages. In winter, he jobs at wood-cart and in carrying stones or gravel for highways; and thus with raising a forest colt or two, provincially called heath-croppers, and one or two of equally inferior species of meat cattle, is found to get on easily, and in some respects independently, through life.

Such a mode of farming was of course anathema to the 'improvers' of the eighteenth and nineteenth centuries. The chapter which follows will consider the changes and developments by which this 'unimproved' agriculture was gradually replaced throughout the region by a much more efficient, scientific, cost- and profit-conscious approach to the whole business of farming.

2. Improvements and developments in agriculture

Farming is often thought of as a conservative and relatively changeless occupation, but although the limitations imposed by soils and climate could not be changed, nonetheless the whole period from 1500 to 1900 saw many developments in the agriculture of the west of England, and witnessed a number of changes which had a profound effect upon rural life and society. Many of the most important changes to be described in this chapter—enclosure and drainage schemes, the watering of meadows, the introduction of new crops, new fertilisers and new methods of stock breeding—were begun by the landlords and gentry who possessed both the capital and the initiative to experiment; but it is the nature of farming innovations that they are available for all to see merely by leaning over a gate, and although farmers were innately cautious, once new ideas had been seen to be profitable and useful most were gradually taken up by the smaller tenant farmers. Some developments were part of the age-old process of agricultural advance, such as the bringing of more land under cultivation, the enclosure of fields and the improvement of rough grazing; these improvements continued throughout the period, though many of the changes, especially the enclosure into individual fields and farms of the great common arable fields of the chalkland area, proceeded most rapidly during the eighteenth and nineteenth centuries. The region did not in general witness the large-scale, depopulating enclosures for the purpose of sheep farming which affected some of the midland counties. The whole subject of enclosures is a very difficult and complicated as well as an emotive subject, and cannot be dealt with fully here. Enclosure meant different things to different people, and did not have the same effect in all areas. There are exceptions to any generalisation about such a large subject, but in general, although some distress was undoubtedly caused by enclosures, and some smaller tenants in the region were dispossessed because of it, most of the evidence suggests that for the region as a whole there is rarely a direct connection between enclosure and depopulation, but that many

24

other factors, such as increase in population, changing farming practice, greater demand for labour from manufacturing areas, must also be taken into account. Another improvement which went on throughout the period was the laborious process of land drainage. Most drainage schemes were small-scale, local affairs, part of the immemorial battle of farmers to win more land for productive use. But a few were more spectacular, particularly the various attempts to drain the Somerset levels, a process which went on throughout the whole period, and continued in the twentieth century. Not all the drainage schemes were successful. For example, during the 1630s a group of Dorset gentlemen, led by the Horseys and Frekes, began work on an ambitious but remarkably ill-conceived project to drain the Fleet, the large expanse of land along the Dorset coast lying between the Chesil beach and the mainland and stretching from Abbotsbury towards Weymouth. This land was covered by salt water at high tide, and during storms the sea also poured over and through the pebbles of the Chesil beach. Vast sums of money were expended upon this scheme, but it inevitably proved a total failure, and it is a great puzzle why it should ever have been thought to be feasible. Sir George Horsey from Clifton Maybank near Sherborne, one of the principal participants, had eventually to admit that the whole idea was unworkable, and that although part of the land

was putt into soe good a way of Drayneinge as that a man with boards fastened to his Feet have gone thereupon . . . neither the same nor any considerable part thereof was made soe Dry or Firme that any profitt might be made thereof, the same for the most parte being in Stormy Weather covered over with Salt Water.

An interesting result of the collapse of this project was that it ruined Sir George Horsey, who was imprisoned for debt in the county gaol at Dorchester where he eventually died in 1640. The family mansion at Clifton Maybank was sold and a large part of it was eventually demolished; during the eighteenth century the front of the house was purchased by the Phelips family and is now incorporated into the west front of their lovely mansion at Montacute.

By far the most important agricultural improvement in the chalkland area was the development of water-meadows. On the chalklands of Wiltshire, Dorset and Hampshire, the water-meadows were the major achievement in agricultural technique during this period, and many thousands of acres of water-meadows may still be seen in the valleys of the chalk streams. These artificially constructed riverside meadows were covered by an elaborate network of channels and hatches which were used to distribute the river-water over the surface of the whole meadow and to drain it off again, thus keeping the meadow covered by a thin, constantly moving sheet of water. The object of a water-meadow was to cover the grass with a thin blanket of running water from the chalk stream, thus maintaining it at a steady temperature, protecting it from frost, and depositing valuable silt and sediment around its roots. This encouraged a much earlier growth of grass than would have occurred naturally, and it enabled those farmers who possessed the necessary capital and enterprise to undertake the expensive business of constructing a water-meadow to break through the most difficult of all barriers to agricultural progress—the age-old problem of insufficient feed for the livestock during the hungry months of the early spring, March and April, when the previous year's hay stocks were exhausted and the natural growth of grass had not yet started. The fast-flowing streams of the Wessex chalkland were ideally suited for the purpose of watering meadows. They were generally not difficult to divert with hatches so as to make them flow over the surface of the meadows; they came direct from the underground reservoirs of the chalk hills and were maintained at a fairly constant temperature, winter and summer alike; and the water was rich in lime which was particularly beneficial for the meadows. Nonetheless, to make a water-meadow necessitated a large capital expenditure, for it involved levelling the surface of the meadow, and weirs and hatches had to be constructed in the main river in order to raise its height so that the water would flow along the channels and trenches which had to be cut with great precision all over the meadow. It was essential that the water should be kept moving over the grass, and that it should not be allowed to lie in pools or to stagnate, since this would kill the grass instead of encouraging its growth. The channels that carried the water across the meadow had to be raised or ridged and made to overflow gently all along their length by a series of subsidiary hatches, so as to maintain a thin sheet of moving water constantly spilling down the sides of the 'panes' or ridges. The water was then collected by a network of drains and returned to the main river. The construction and operation of this system demanded great expertise, and the 'waterman' or 'drowner' who managed the meadows and controlled the flow of water over them became an important figure in the chalkland areas. It is not clear just how or where the idea originated, and it seems likely that it was developed gradually in several places. Certainly the idea spread very rapidly indeed during the seventeenth century along the valleys of the Avon and Wylye in Wiltshire, the Frome and Piddle in Dorset and the Test and Itchen in Hampshire. There are references to water-meadows as early as 1608 in the court rolls of Affpuddle on the river Piddle in Dorset, and in 1629 a 'waterman' was appointed by the whole manor to control the watering of all the common meadows, and the tenants agreed to pay his wages. In 1629 the tenants assembled in the manorial court at Puddletown, three miles up the valley from Affpuddle, reached an agreement for 'wateringe and Improvinge theire groundes', and for carrying out all the necessary work to water their meadows. The idea of water-meadows rapidly spread along the chalkland streams of Dorset, such as the Frome, Piddle, Cerne, Tarrant and Gussage, and water-meadows were also established on the Stour. By 1659 the idea and techniques were already well established, and when in that year the lord and tenants of Charlton Marshall on the river Stour near Blandford Forum decided to make a water-meadow they were able to send to Tolpuddle in the Piddle valley for two 'able and sufficient carpenters' to make the hatches, and to nearby Turners Puddle for Henry Phelps 'a known Antient, Able and well-Experienced waterman' who was to supervise the whole project, 'soe ordering the water whereby the said groundes might be well watered'. Water-meadows were certainly established in the Wylye valley in Wiltshire during the 1630s and John Aubrey, who remembered the first watering of meadows at Wylye and Chalke about the year 1635, later wrote that

The improvement of watering meadows began at Wylye, about 1635, about which time, I remember, we began to use them at Chalke. Watering of meadows about Marleburgh and so to Hungerford was, I remember, about 1646, and Mr John Bayly, of Bishop's Down, near Salisbury, about the same time made his great improvements by watering there by St Thomas's Bridge.

There are also early references to watering meadows at Shalbourne, Broad Hinton, Damerham, Downton Newcourt and Chilmark. Water-meadows had spread into Hampshire by the second half of the seventeenth century, and were commonplace there along the Test and Itchen by 1700.

It is noticeable that the early development of water-meadows owed much to the active encouragement of energetic landlords. When the tenants at Wylye agreed to water their meadows in 1632, the Earl of Pembroke's steward presided over the meeting of the manorial court at which the decision was taken; the introduction of water-meadows at Affpuddle and the surrounding area was firmly supported by the lord of the manor, Sir Edward Lawrence, who was keenly interested in agricultural improvement; and at Puddletown in October 1629 when the tenants met to decide about watering their meadows the manorial court book records that

The honorable Henrie Hastings esquire Lord of the same manor being present with the Tenants of the same and a great debate beinge theare had and questions moved by some of the tenants about wateringe and Improvinge theire groundes and theare heard att large, And thereupon by Full consent yt was ordered in Courte and agreed unto by the tenants in court . . . .

The water-meadows continued in use throughout the eighteenth and nineteenth centuries, and were of incalculable importance in the agriculture of the chalkland districts. The principal advantage which derived from the water-meadows was that they provided early feed for the sheep flocks, and so made it possible to keep much larger flocks than would otherwise have been possible. This in turn meant that more sheep were available for folding on the arable land, thus greatly increasing its productiveness, so that the real profit from the water-meadows emerged in the improved corn crops. The meadows also provided an abundant crop of hay, and thereafter they could also be used for the dairy cattle in the later summer and autumn, before being prepared for the next winter's watering. In those manors where water-meadows were established, the sheep flocks followed a regular calendar of grazing and folding throughout the year. The meadows were generally flooded or 'drowned' for varying periods from early October to Christmas, depending on the weather and often also on complicated agreements with other manors in the same valley and with millers about the use of the water. Meanwhile the sheep were pastured on the downland by day and folded on the wheat or fallows at night. The meadows would be given further periods of watering after Christmas, especially during times of frost, so that by Lady Day of even earlier in mild winters, there would be sufficient growth of grass for the sheep to feed on them for short periods each day. This was the period when the water-meadows really proved their value, when the downland grazing was exhausted and before the natural growth of grass had started. The sheep were folded straight from the meadows on to the land destined for barley, since then the dung and urine of the flock was particularly valuable. Often the fold was continued after the barley was sown, providing both top-dressing and consolidation of the land, and even after the corn had appeared, another folding would encourage stronger growth. The water-meadows were unsuitable for the sheep after the beginning of May, since then they were likely to contract liver fluke and foot-rot from the damp pasture. But by this time the meadows would in any case have been eaten bare, and the natural downland grazing would be available for the sheep. The water-meadows could be flooded for a few days and thereafter left for hay. Again the possession of a water-meadow was an enormous advantage, since a floated meadow could produce up to four times as much hay as unwatered land, and the crop could be gained in spite of drought; in addition the water-meadows never needed to be manured. The water-meadows were generally used for cattle grazing during July, August and September; but cattle could only be fed in them during these months since earlier, in wetter conditions, they would 'poach' the ground and damage the channels. After Michaelmas the water-meadows were cleared of stock and the channels, hatches and sluices were cleaned out and repaired, so that the meadows were ready for the winter flooding. Thomas Davis writing on the agriculture of Wiltshire in 1794 considered the value of the water-meadows 'almost incalculable', and concluded that 'the water-meadows of Wiltshire and the neighbouring counties, are a branch of husbandry that can never be too much recommended'. Similarly, John Claridge in his Report to the Board of Agriculture on the farming of Dorset in 1793 wrote of the water-meadows, 'the early vegetation produced by flooding, is of such consequence to the Dorsetshire farmer, that without it, their present system of managing sheep would be about annihilated'.

Several factors led to the decline of the water-meadows and to the disuse of most of them at the end of the nineteenth century and during the twentieth century. The severe slump in agriculture during the period after 1870 led to many changes in farming practice and to the disappearance of many of the great sheep flocks. The introduction of artificial fertilisers, improved strains of grasses and alternative sources of early spring feed for livestock also made the water-meadows less indispensable than they had been. Finally, the cost of the skilled labour required for the maintenance and management of the meadows, and the fact that they could not easily be worked by machinery or with tractors, all led to the abandonment of the meadows, many of which are still easily recognisable but now present a sorry picture of neglect and decay. But for much of the period here under review, they were 'the crowning glory of agricultural achievement', and were an indispensable factor in the farming pattern of the chalkland parts of the region.

The four centuries from 1500 to 1900 also witnessed the introduction and popularisation of a whole range of new crops in the farms of the region. Many of these were connected with various local industries, such as the hemp and flax which were grown in several places, especially in west Dorset and south Somerset, and which supplied the rope, net and sailcloth industries of Bridport, Crewkerne, Coker, Beaminster and the surrounding district. Various dye-stuffs were also grown, particularly woad and madder for use by the cloth industry of the region. Woad, for example, was much grown in the area around Cranborne on the Wiltshire-Dorset border, and in various places in Somerset, including the Keynsham area and Cheddar. Teazles were also extensively grown in Somerset, especially in the north of the county in Wrington, Blagdon, Ubley, Compton Martin and parts of the Chew valley; the teazles were used in the cloth industry for raising the nap on the cloth during the finishing process. During the late eighteenth and early nineteenth centuries large quantities of teazles produced in the area were sent by ship from Bristol to Yorkshire for use in the cloth industry there. Other introductions were mainly of fodder crops, which, like the water-meadows, enabled a larger number of livestock to be kept. These included turnips and carrots which had long been grown in gardens and became common field crops in the region from the eighteenth century onwards, especially in the rich soils of the vale of Taunton Deane, in the vale of Pewsey and in the area of greensand around Yeovil and Crewkerne. Rape, clover, rye-grass and other grasses, and sainfoin also spread throughout the region during the eighteenth century; clover seed was on sale in the markets of the south-west from the late seventeenth century onwards. Edward Lisle, who farmed at Crux Easton in Hampshire near the border with Wiltshire and Berkshire during the late seventeenth and early eighteenth centuries, wrote that clover, rye-grass and sainfoin had been grown in that area for nearly 50 years; John Aubrey writing in 1685 noted that sainfoin was first introduced at North Wraxall, in that area between Bath and Chippenham where the Cotswolds push into Wiltshire, by Nicholas Hall, a farmer who had come there from Dundry in Somerset about 1650. It is noticeable, however, that Aubrey mentions the turnip only as a garden vegetable.

Cabbages, which had long been known as a garden vegetable, were said by several seventeenth-century writers to have been first grown as a field crop to provide feed for stock by Sir Anthony Ashley of Wimborne St Giles in Dorset, who introduced the idea from Holland during the early seventeenth century. Ashley died in 1627, and his elaborate tomb in the church at Wimborne St Giles has what is reputed to be the representation of a cabbage at his feet. This consists of a stone sphere, about 9 in. in diameter, covered by a pattern of hexagonal shapes.

From the seventeenth century improved varieties and strains of wheat, barley, oats and rye, as well as new methods of cultivation and crop rotation, gradually increased the yields from these traditional crops. The large-scale growth of the potato as a field crop was a comparatively late development in the region, but from the late eighteenth century onwards potatoes were being grown extensively, and were used for animal feeding as well as becoming a very important element in human diet, particularly for the poor, and especially in the years of very high corn prices during the Napoleonic Wars. Thomas Davis, writing on Wiltshire farming in 1794, noted that

Potatoes have of late been very much cultivated in all parts of this district, but particularly on the sandy lands. The general introduction of this valuable root, has been exceedingly fortunate for the labouring poor, of whose sustenance they now make a very considerable part, especially in the season when wheat is dear.

William Stevenson in 1812 wrote of Dorset that the potato had only been introduced into gardens some 30 or 40 years previously, but that by the early nineteenth century it was being grown very widely as a field crop all over the county, and especially on the rich soils of the western part in the neighbourhood of Abbotsbury, Bridport and Beaminster. Likewise John Billingsley writing on the cultivation of potatoes in north Somerset in 1795 reported that

The rapid extension of the cultivation of this root can only be equalled by its general utility as a food for man and beast. Thirty or forty years ago it was an extraordinary thing to see an acre of potatoes in one spot, and in one man's possession; now there are many parishes in this district which can produce fifty acres.

During the nineteenth century the potato became a vital element in the food of the farm labourers for, as will be shown in the following chapters, it was not only in Ireland that the potato saved many of the population from starvation.

New methods of cultivation, of fertilisation and of crop rotation, which spread gradually during the eighteenth and early nineteenth centuries, particularly under the stimulus of the high corn prices during the Napoleonic Wars, also had the effect of increasing production tremendously. The new methods included the use of iron equipment in place of the traditional wooden ploughs, or 'sulls' as they were called in the west country, and harrows, as well as the new drills and threshing and winnowing machines. Large areas of chalk downland were broken up for arable, especially during the later nineteenth century when the steam-plough became available and made massive inroads on the downs. Methods of land-drainage were greatly improved, especially with the spread of cheap clay drainage-pipes, many of them made in Bridgwater. Drainage also brought large areas of the Somerset levels into productive agricultural use. John Billingsley reported in 1795 that a vast improvement had been made in what he called the 'Somerset Waterlands' by recent drainage work, and he enthusiastically recommended landowners to press ahead with further drainage schemes. From the seventeenth century onwards, increasing quantities of marl and lime were used to improve the fertility of the soil, as well as ashes, soot, rags, tanning waste and all sorts of industrial refuse. It was the chalkland region, the traditional corn-growing area, which had always suffered most from a shortage of manure. This was partly because the chalkland soils needed great quantities of manure if they were to grow satisfactory crops of corn, and partly because of the practice, which had long been traditional in that comparatively treeless area, of burning cow-dung dried in the sun as fuel. The Cornish traveller and writer, Peter Mundy, who travelled through Dorset and Wiltshire in 1635 wrote that 'For Fewell they use Cowdung, Kneaded and tempred with short strawe or strawe dust, which they make into flatt Cakes and Clapping them on the side of their stoney walls, they become dry and hard, and soe they use them when they have occasion.' This custom continued in some places, for example on the island of Portland, which is almost completely devoid of trees, as well as in other parts of the chalkland, until well into the nineteenth century. William Barnes, the Dorset dialect poet of the nineteenth century, in a poem on the benefits which a village could derive from a piece of common land wrote that

> An when the children be too young to earn
> A penny, they can g'out in sunny weather,
> An' run about, an' get together
> A bag o' cow-dung vor to burn.

Until the advent of cheap artificial fertilisers therefore, and even with the advantages of the sheep-fold, it was very difficult to obtain adequate manure for the chalkland arable. This led to all sorts of expedients. On the island of Portland, for example, a practice continued for many years which was known as Chamber-Lye. This was described in the early nineteenth century in the following terms:

In the Isle of Portland they have a practice of long standing, of preserving all the urine that is made in winter, carrying it out in casks, and distributing it over the wheat crops, in a manner somewhat similar to that used in watering the streets of large towns. This kind of manure has been found to answer well . . . .

In other places all sorts of substitutes for animal fertilisers were tried: soot, rags, night-soil from towns, industrial waste, etc. and, in some places along the coast, sea-weed and even fish were used to enhance the fertility of the soil.

In this, as in so many other aspects of rural life, the coming of the railways in the nineteenth century had a dramatic effect, making readily and cheaply available in most parts of the region supplies of artificial fertiliser. It was this fact which was to dislodge the sheep flocks from their age-old position as the lynch-pin of chalkland agriculture. The railways also brought cheap drainage-pipes and the new mass-produced farm implements, thus also paving the way for an expansion of arable farming in the clayland areas. Evidence of the enthusiasm for agricultural improvement and innovation which existed in the region during the late eighteenth and early nineteenth centuries is seen in the formation of various agricultural clubs and societies for the purpose of spreading information and encouraging higher standards among farmers. Some of these were small, local societies, but pre-eminent in the west-country was the Bath and West of England Society which was founded at Bath in 1777. The influence of the Bath and West Society was felt far and wide throughout the region in its shows, meetings, lectures, practical demonstrations and publications. It was one important factor in bringing about a steady growth in the efficiency and productivity of arable farming in the region, and the gradual introduction of new crops and new techniques. Some of the most spectacular of the agricultural improvements occurred with livestock and these will be described in the following section.

LIVESTOCK FARMING

Few farmers in the west of England during the sixteenth and seventeenth centuries paid much attention to the selective breeding or improvement of livestock, and most of the cattle, sheep and pigs were an indiscriminate mixture of breeds. But during the eighteenth and nineteenth centuries tremendous strides were made in this branch of farming. One aspect of livestock in the region, which may be dealt with at the outset, was the improvement in the breeds of horses during the period, and the replacement of oxen by horses. Horses had already taken the place of oxen over most of the chalkland by 1500, both for pulling the plough and for drawing carts, but on the heavier soils of the clayland most of the ploughing and heavy work continued for another two centuries to be done by oxen, and in many places oxen continued in use through the nineteenth century. The shallow, light soils of most of the chalkland areas could be ploughed satisfactorily by the small, agile horses of the region in the early part of the period, but until the coming of heavier, stronger and better-bred horses in the eighteenth century, the clinging clay soils needed the slower but steady strong pull of an ox-team for the plough.

New breeds of sheep more productive of wool and mutton were developed as an alternative to the old Wiltshire and Dorset 'Horn' breeds, and during the early nineteenth century many farmers experimented with crosses of Southdowns and Leicesters, while later in the century the Hampshire and Dorset 'Down' breeds emerged. Improvements were also made in the 'Horn' breeds which continued to be kept in large numbers throughout the region. The early nineteenth century also saw much experimentation in the breeding of cattle and the emergence of several new breeds. New crosses based on the old Longhorns and on the Devonshire, Gloucester and Hereford breeds were introduced, and, later, on the Shorthorns, Ayrshires and Suffolks.

Great improvements were also made in the old breeds of pigs, with the introduction of Chinese and other crosses, and the west of England saw the notable emergence of the 'Wessex Saddleback', based on the hardy, black pig of the Hampshire forest area. This pig became very popular throughout the region: growing rapidly and fattening easily, it was admirably suited to the needs of the dairy farmers.

For much of the nineteenth century agriculture throughout the region was of a very high standard, and many farmers were very prosperous although, as will be shown in Chapter 4, this prosperity did not extend to the farm labourers. But there is no doubt of the excellence of much of the farming, with intensive cultivation, adoption of new methods and implements, high yields both of arable crops and of milk and fat sheep and cattle. William Cobbett, who was by no means an uncritical observer, enthused over the farming of much of the Hampshire and Wiltshire chalkland, and found the agriculture of the Avon valley in Wiltshire as fine as anything he had seen on any of his Rural Rides. He wrote in August 1826 that,

I delight in this sort of country; and I had frequently seen the vale of the Itchen, that of the Bourn, and also that of the Test in Hampshire; I had seen the vales amongst the South Downs; but I never before saw anything to please me like this valley of the Avon. I sat upon my horse and looked over Milton and Easton and Pewsey for half an hour, though I had not breakfasted.

Another perceptive observer, L. H. Ruegg, the editor of a Dorset local paper, in an essay on the Farming of Dorsetshire published by the Royal Agricultural Society in 1854 wrote that the standard of farming throughout the county was as high as any in England—'from Woodyates to six miles beyond Dorchester (nearly the entire length of the chalk district) there is no better farming in the Kingdom.'

Many enthusiastic agricultural 'improvers' had contributed to raising the standards of all branches of farming, particularly during the time of high prices which coincided with the Napoleonic Wars, a period at which many farming fortunes were founded. Arthur Young, the enthusiastic advocate of improved farming methods, in a tour through the whole region in 1771, noted not only many areas where there was great scope for improvement, but also many places where much experiment and many new methods were being tried. For example, in Dorset he was delighted with the work he saw being carried out on the estates of Humphrey Sturt of Crichell, who was experimenting with land reclamation and drainage on the heathland, and had introduced the cultivation of sainfoin, lucerne, buckwheat and carrots; he had also started a scheme to turn Brownsea island in Poole harbour into productive agricultural land. For the latter purpose Sturt was employing barges to bring dung, soap ashes and other manures from London, Portsmouth and Poole. Also in Dorset, Young noted the improvements being carried out by William Frampton at Moreton, John Damer at Came near Dorchester, and especially by Lord Milton at Milton Abbas—'The public is not a little indebted to this nobleman for attending with so much propriety to the improvement of the husbandry of Dorsetshire.' Young was particularly struck by the success of William White, whose career illustrates very well the opportunities which existed for a conscientious man prepared to work very hard, and who was blessed with a hard-working family and good luck. White had started life as a farm labourer, but by exceptional diligence and thrift had managed to save enough to rent a small piece of poor, ill-drained land on the edge of the heath from William Frampton of Moreton. By working all the hours he could and by his skill with cattle he had prospered greatly and gradually acquired the lease of 120 acres from Frampton, 16 acres of which he had reclaimed from the heath by his own labours. His success was accomplished through amazingly hard work and in spite of some set-backs, including a disastrous fire which destroyed all his farmstead. But White had refused to be daunted, and had immediately set about rebuilding his house and farm buildings with his own hands, becoming his own mason, carpenter and thatcher. Above all he attributed his success to his use of water-meadows. After talking to him, Young wrote that 'Bringing water over all the land that he possibly could, has been the principal means of his general success with grass land.' This enabled him to keep twice as many cattle as his neighbours, and to raise himself from a day-labourer to being a substantial farmer. White's story is no doubt exceptional, but does illustrate what could be achieved by an energetic man in a period of agricultural expansion.

Many parts of Somerset also witnessed an agricultural revolution during the late eighteenth and early nineteenth century. In the rich lands of the vale of Taunton Deane, always in the forefront of agricultural progress, new methods, new implements and new crops were introduced including the cultivation of new fodder crops such as lucerne, sainfoin, burnet and timothy grass, and the use of the drill for sowing corn and peas and beans. In heavy soils of this area oxen continued to be used as plough beasts until well into the nineteenth century. In the grazing-lands around Bridgwater and inland across the Somerset levels new breeds and crosses of cattle had a great effect on milk-yields and on the quality of the beef steers that were produced, just as the continuing drainage-works brought many more acres into productive use. The man whose name is chiefly linked with the pioneering of agricultural improvements in Somerset is John Billingsley (1747–1811). Billingsley lived throughout his life at Ashwick Grove, on the Mendips near Shepton Mallet. He was an active member of the Bath and West of England Society and worked hard to spread the knowledge of improved agricultural methods. Above all, he is remembered as the author of the 'General View of the Agriculture of Somerset' which he wrote for the recently-formed Board of Agriculture in 1794. In this he made an eloquent plea for greater progress in land drainage and reclamation, enclosures, better roads, the construction of canals, improved farming implements, crops, varieties and techniques, and every possible device for increasing the fertility and productivity of the land. His book also contains the memorable picture of the traditional smallholder, under-employed on his unproductive acres, and dependent upon the feed provided by an overstocked piece of common grazing land, and of the benefits which Billingsley alleges would follow from enclosure and a more profit-conscious and efficient approach to farming:

. . . moral effects of an injurious tendency accrue to the cottager, from a reliance on the imaginery benefits of stocking a common. The possession of a cow or two, with a hog, and a few geese, naturally exalts the peasant in his own conception above his brethren in the same rank of society. It inspires some degree of confidence in a property, inadequate to his support. In sauntering after his cattle, he acquires a habit of indolence. Quarter, half and occasionally whole days are imperceptibly lost. Day-labour becomes disgusting; the aversion increases by indulgence and, at length, the sale of a half-fed calf, or hog, finishes the means of adding intemperance to idleness. The sale of the cow frequently succeeds, and its wretched and disappointed possessor, unwilling to resume the daily and regular course of labour, from whence he drew his former subsistence, by various modes of artifice and imposition, exacts from the poor's-rate that relief to which he is in no degree entitled.

This description is by no means exaggerated. The parish of Wedmore, which abounded with cottage commons, and one of the largest and most opulent in this county, will illustrate its truth and justice. Within twenty years there have been enclosed upwards of three thousand acres of rich moor land, heretofore, when in commons, rendered unproductive by inundations and their consequence, six or seven months in the year, and when passable for the remaining months, of little value from being overstocked; which land is now let, with liberal allowance of profit to the occupier, from thirty to sixty shillings per acre. These enclosures are made by ditches, which by annual cleaning and spreading the contents over the surface, afford an excellent manure, with a new and extensive source of labour of the most productive kind, whereby the poor's-rate has been reduced, or at least has not exceeded its former amount. . . .

In Wiltshire also there were many farmers eager to adopt and profit from the improved methods of farming which became available during the nineteenth century. For example the Stratton family, who rose from being small dairy farmers in the Pewsey Vale at the beginning of the century to become among the largest and most progressive farmers in the county by 1870. They were enthusiastic 'improvers'; became noted breeders of prize-winning Shorthorn cows, and are reputed to have introduced into the county the first mowing-machine, the first steam threshing-machine and the first steam-plough. R. Rawlence and E. P. Squarey were both active farmers in the county, as well as the founders of a firm of land agents. Both farmed on a very large scale in the south of the county, as well as being actively concerned with fostering and financing agricultural improvements. Wiltshire was also in the forefront of the invention and introduction of new kinds of agricultural machinery and implements, with firms such as Robert and John Reeves of Bratton, Brown and May of Devizes, J. W. Titt of Warminster, and many others who produced improved ploughs, threshing-machines, elevators and other implements, as well as steam-engines both for threshing and for steam ploughing.

Much of the agricultural prosperity of the region came to an end during the 1870s. Several factors contributed to the severe depression in farming which lasted until 1914 and was marked by rapidly declining prices for farm produce and by very great hardship and distress among farmers, many of whom went out of business or were forced to alter radically the whole pattern of their farming. The causes of this slump included a succession of wet, cold springs and summers, followed inevitably by disastrously poor harvests, particularly in the appallingly bad year 1879. These years of very poor grain yields coincided with a drop in corn prices which followed the influx of cheap corn from the United States and Canada. The price of

37

corn fell dramatically; for example in 1847 wheat had sold at 70 shillings per quarter; by 1870 the price had already fallen in the face of foreign competition to 46 shillings, and by 1894 it was down to 24 shillings per quarter. The low prices and poor corn harvests naturally hit hardest the farmers on the chalklands of Hampshire, Dorset and Wiltshire who were dependent upon corn-growing for the greater part of their livelihood. Between 1870 and 1890 the acreages of wheat and barley grown throughout the chalklands of the three counties shrank by more than 25 per cent, as more and more arable land was laid down to grass; and chalkland farmers were further hit by the sharp fall in the price of wool during these years. The wet seasons produced a foot-rot which ravaged sheep flocks in Hampshire, Dorset and Wiltshire; and the decline in the corn acreage also caused a drop in the number of sheep, since the sheep flocks' primary use had been to maintain the fertility of the arable land by folding. In Dorset the number of sheep kept in the county declined between 1870 and 1900 by nearly 40 per cent; and in Wiltshire during the period from 1880 to 1900 the number of sheep dropped by more than one fifth. This decline continued throughout the first half of the twentieth century, and between 1880 and 1950 the sheep numbers in Wiltshire had dropped by no less than 90 per cent. The decline in the number of sheep, together with the increased availability of artificial fertilisers and of new, improved strains of grasses, also caused many farmers to abandon their water-meadows, and began the process whereby almost all the water-meadows in the region have gone out of use.

The effects of the slump in farming were not confined to the chalklands, but were also felt in the dairy farming, stock-rearing areas of the claylands, where grassland predominated and corn-growing was of minor importance. The clayland farmers were also badly hit by the run of wet, cold summers which caused liver-rot among the cattle, made it difficult to produce sufficient good-quality hay for the winters, and led to a decline in milk production. Moreover, imports of American cheese brought a dramatic fall in prices during the period 1878–80 and caused many farmers, especially those within reach of the railways, to turn from cheese and butter production to the sale of liquid milk. This in turn affected the number of pigs which could be kept on the farms, since previously they had been fed partly on the whey from cheese-making. The change to liquid-milk production also accelerated the decline of the old longhorn breed of cows which had been favoured by cheesemakers in favour of the larger milk-yields of the Dairy Shorthorn breed which by 1900 had become by far the most common kind of cow kept throughout the region.

Other aspects of clayland farming also suffered badly from the slump. The hemp- and flax-growing of Somerset and Dorset declined sharply in the face of foreign competition so that, for example, whereas in 1873 there were 712 acres of flax grown in Dorset, by 1881 the acreage had fallen to 225, and by 1884 had dropped to 117 acres; in 1894 the acreage had shrunk to a mere 25 acres and by 1900 the cultivation of flax in the county had ceased altogether. A similar decline is also seen in the hemp and flax grown in Somerset.

Landlords were also affected by the inability of their tenants to pay an economic rent because of the slump, so that by 1895 a Royal Commission enquiring into agricultural distress in the region reported of Dorset that 'Ownership of agricultural land is rapidly becoming a luxury which only men possessing other sources of income can enjoy.' The total effect of such a disastrous and extended period of agricultural depression upon a region so dependent upon farming was immense. Other results of the slump—the decline in the demand for farm labour, the social difficulties this caused, the rapid decline in the population of almost every town and village in the region between 1870 and 1900, the decay of many of those trades and industries which depended upon agriculture—will all be considered in the following chapters.

3. Rural industries

Although agriculture was the main occupation of most people in Wessex during the period from 1500 to 1900, nonetheless a large part of the rural population of the area also engaged in one or more secondary occupations, or by-employments, and for a few it was industry which provided their main livelihood and farming which was secondary. Apart from industries such as quarrying or mining, which depended upon the local occurrence of minerals or suitable stone, other industries and by-employments were generally grouped in particular parts of the region where raw materials or traditional skills were to be found, or, perhaps most important of all, where the pattern of farming provided the necessary free time.

By far the most important industry throughout the whole region for most of the period was cloth-making. This was an ancient, traditional industry in the region, but during the early middle ages it had been confined to the towns like Bristol, Salisbury, Malmesbury, Marlborough and Devizes, and it was not until the introduction of the fulling-mill in the later middle ages that the industry spread to the banks of fast-running streams and into the countryside; and at the same time began to expand to serve a national and international market rather than purely local needs. This expansion illustrates very clearly that it was not the existence of local supplies of wool which was the vital factor in the establishment of a cloth industry, but that plentiful labour was much more important. Wool could fairly easily be transported, and the wool of the chalkland sheep of Wiltshire, Dorset and Hampshire was not in any case of the highest quality; it is no accident therefore that the main centres of the cloth industry were not in the chalklands or the Cotswolds where the great flocks of sheep were kept, but were in the clayland areas of north Wiltshire, along the west Wiltshire border at Bradford-on-Avon, Trowbridge, Westbury, Steeple Ashton, Warminster and many other places, and across the Somerset border along the valley of the river Frome, including Frome, Beckington, Rode, Norton St Philip, Hinton Charterhouse, Bath, Keynsham and

Shepton Mallet. Other important areas of the cloth trade were in the Taunton and Wellington district of Somerset and in the clay vales of west Dorset, from Sherborne through Beaminster and Broadwindsor towards Lyme Regis. These were all areas of pastoral farming with comparatively little arable land, and were composed mainly of small dairy farmers, making butter and cheese, a type of farming which allowed time to engage in secondary employments—spinning, weaving, fulling and dyeing. In the chalkland areas, where arable farming predominated, and where the fertility of the land was maintained by the folding of the great sheep flocks, the cloth industry was of minor importance, for arable farming gave much less opportunity for engaging in by-employments. The Somerset J.P.'s during the early seventeenth century evidently well understood the sort of countryside in which handicraft industries could flourish, when they reported to the Privy Council upon the eastern part of Somerset that 'a great part of it being forest and woodlands and the rest very barren for corn . . . the people of the country (for the most part) being occupied about the trade of clothmaking, spinning, weaving and tucking.' Earlier, the antiquarian traveller John Leland who journeyed through west Wiltshire in about 1542 had been greatly impressed by the scale and importance of the woollen industry and wrote for example of Bradford-on-Avon that 'Al the toune of Bradeford stondith by clooth making', and of Trowbridge that it was 'very welle buildid of stone, and florishith by drapery'. Leland made similar comments on most of the towns of west Wiltshire and also on many of the little towns and villages of the eastern and north-eastern parts of Somerset, as for example of Pensford on the river Chew where he wrote that 'It is a praty market townlet occupied with clothing' and 'The towne stondith much by clothing', or at Chew Magna 'There hath beene good makyng of cloth yn the towne'. The most famous of all the sixteenth-century clothiers of Wiltshire was William Stumpe of Malmesbury whom Leland described as 'an exceding riche clothiar'. At the dissolution of the monasteries, Stumpe had purchased from the Crown the whole site of Malmesbury Abbey with the abbey buildings. Inside the abbey he built a mansion for himself and filled 'every corner of the vaste houses of office that belonged to the abbay . . . (with) . . . lumbes to weve clooth yn'. Most of the cloth made in the region during the sixteenth century was the heavy broadcloth, and much of the production was exported, generally undyed, to be finished on the continent. The Dorset ports—Poole, Weymouth and Lyme Regis, had a flourishing trade in cloth exports, shipping to the continent not only cloth produced in Dorset but also cloth from south Somerset, Chard, Crewkerne and district and from Taunton, Minehead and as far as Barnstaple. Lyme Regis had a considerable export trade during the seventeenth century in poorer quality woollen fabrics known as 'Kerseys' and 'dozens'. Many of these cloths were exported to France— especially to Brittany and Normandy where, it was said, they were purchased by poor people 'of a base disposicion who would not go to the price of a good clothe'. Much of the cloth produced in Wiltshire and in the Frome area was, however, sent by packhorse to London to be sold at Blackwell Hall either to be dyed and finished by London merchants for the home market, or to be sent abroad.

During the later sixteenth century, the production of lighter cloths, the 'new draperies' began to expand in the region, as well as 'medley cloth' for which the wool was dyed before spinning. For this cloth fine-quality Spanish wool was used, and by the early seventeenth century the manufacture of 'Spanish cloth' was well established. It was not only the business of weaving and tucking or fulling which provided employment in the region, but each weaver had to be supplied with yarn by the work of many spinners, and throughout much of the period spinning was the most important and universal (secondary) employment in the whole region. John Hooker's description of the situation in Devon in 1600 would have applied with equal force to most of the region, that 'wheresoever any man doth travel you shall fynde at the hall dore as they do name the foredore of the house, he shall I saye fynde the wiffe, theire children and theire servants at the turne spynninge or at theire cardes cardinge and by which commoditie the common people doe lyve'.

In the early eighteenth century Defoe was greatly impressed by the size and extent of the woollen industry and by the number of people employed in it. He commented that to see the quantity of wool sold in the market, it would not seem 'possible to be consumed, manufactured, and wrought up'; but on the other hand 'those that saw the numbers of people imploy'd, and the vast quantity of goods made in this part of England, would wonder where the whole nation such be able to supply them with wooll'. The woollen industry continued to be the most important single employer of labour apart from agriculture until the nineteenth century, and during the Napoleonic Wars experienced a boom, since the revolutionary wars disrupted the industry on the continent and effectively removed foreign competition. An example of the fortunes to be made in the textile trade during the early nineteenth century is to be seen in the firm of J. & T. Clark of Trowbridge, two brothers who started in business in 1801 with a capital of £500 lent to them by an uncle. By hard work and business enterprise they prospered greatly in the conditions created by the war, and by the time the war ended in 1815 the firm was worth £10,929.

It was during the Napoleonic Wars that new machinery began to take the place of the old hand-methods in the industry. The first spinning jenny, a machine which was to revolutionise the process of spinning and deprive many people in the region of their traditional work, was introduced at Shepton Mallet as early as 1776. Its appearance provoked a riot in which many people from Wiltshire and the Frome valley also took part. It was not for another ten years that spinning jennies and carding machines began to be common in the region, and there was still considerable opposition to them. There was, for example, a riot at Bradford-on-Avon in 1791 over the introduction of a carding machine, and the offending instrument was burned by the mob. The flying shuttle which was to mechanise the weaving process also caused great disturbances when it first appeared. For example, there were serious riots at Trowbridge in 1792 which had to be quelled by the militia, and its use in the region came about very slowly and in the face of great resistance from the work force.

After 1815 the west of England woollen industry went into a steep decline from which it was never fully to recover and which was to lead eventually to the virtual disappearance of the trade. There were many reasons for this. Much of the industry clung to an old traditional cloth of very high quality which was unable to stand up to the competition of the cheaper mass-produced cloths of the North of England; and especially could not compete with a flood of cheap cotton goods. Moreover the west of England was in general slow to adopt new methods and new machinery. During the nineteenth century, therefore, the history of the industry in the region is one of decline and recession, of mills closing, fewer men employed and a steady contraction of output.

Besides the woollen industry, some other textiles have had an importance in providing employment in various parts of the region. Among these have been silk-weaving which was introduced into the area around Sherborne and Yeovil in the middle of the seventeenth century, and at the same time into various parts of Wiltshire, including Salisbury, Warminster and Malmesbury. This industry became very important during the eighteenth century and continued throughout the nineteenth century to employ great numbers of people both in mills and as out-workers. The Sherborne silk mill continues in use, but by an appropriate progression it has now been turned over to the processing of fibre-glass.

The manufacture of lace provided work for many people from the sixteenth to the nineteenth century, and was carried on in many parts of the region, notably around Lyme Regis and at Blandford Forum in Dorset, and at Salisbury and Marlborough in Wiltshire. Lace-making was ideal as a by-employment for women and girls and could easily be combined with other jobs; John Aubrey wrote in 1680 that 'our shepherdesses of late years do begin to work point whereas before they did only knit coarse stockings'; and Defoe noted that Blandford Forum was

a handsome well-built town, but chiefly famous for making the finest bonelace in England, and where they shew'd me some so exquisitely fine, as I think I never saw better in Flanders, France or Italy . . . .

This industry was finally killed by the competition of machine-made lace in the nineteenth century.

In parts of south Somerset and west Dorset the production of linen and sail-cloth was an important industry throughout the whole period. It depended very largely on locally grown flax which flourished in the rich soils of that area, though during the nineteenth century both flax and hemp were imported. The industry was centred around Crewkerne, East and West Coker and Chard in Somerset, and Beaminster, Broadwindsor and Bridport in Dorset. Originally dependent upon locally grown hemp was the rope, net, thread and webbing industry of the Bridport area. The rich soils of the Marshwood vale were highly suitable for growing hemp, and the industry was established at Bridport early in the middle ages. During the sixteenth and seventeenth centuries the town supplied ropes and nets to the Newfoundland fishing fleets which operated from the Dorset ports, as well as fulfilling the needs of the Royal Navy and of other merchant shipping. Thomas Fuller, author of *The Worthies of England* who was rector of Broadwindsor in west Dorset from 1634 to 1641, commented on the widespread cultivation of hemp in the area, and wrote that 'England hath no better than what groweth here betwixt Beaminster and Bridport, our land affording so much strong and deep ground proper for the same . . .' His evidence is supported by the field-names of west Dorset, where in almost every parish there are closes bearing names such as Hemphay, Hemp Close, Hemp Lands as well as Flax Close, Flaxlands and Flecklands. Hemp and flax both required a great deal of care in their cultivation, and both demanded laborious preparation before they could be spun. These tasks as well as the work of weaving, net- and rope-making, etc. all provided a great deal of employment in the scattered farms and cottages of west Dorset and south Somerset.

These industries continued throughout the eighteenth and nineteenth centuries, and although the local production of the raw materials has ceased, they continue in the twentieth century, using imported hemp and flax as well as man-made fibres.

The Wessex region is remarkable for the diversity of its geological structures and the variety of its stone, and it is not surprising therefore that stone-quarrying has been an important industry in many places where the local stone was suitable for building work. Until the eighteenth and nineteenth centuries when easy means of transport became available, most quarries supplied only local needs, for only exceptionally fine stone was worth the hard labour and high costs involved in carrying it very far from the quarry. It was largely because the stone could be easily carried by sea that two places along the Dorset coast possessed the most important of all the quarries in the region and that their stone enjoyed a national reputation. These were the quarries of Purbeck and Portland. The period of the national fame and importance of Purbeck stone or 'marble' had occurred during the thirteenth and fourteenth centuries, when it was used in the construction and decoration of churches and other buildings all over England, and was also extremely popular for monumental effigies. By the sixteenth century, because of the decline in church-building and the growth in the popularity of Derbyshire alabaster and other materials for monuments, the demand for the high-quality Purbeck stone had fallen off; but stone continued to be quarried there and the industry remained an important employer of labour, because of the demand for the poorer quality stone from the upper beds, which was cut out in slabs and used for roofing and paving. Much of this stone was sent by sea to London from Poole, Swanage and the little port of Ower, and this continued to be the main use of Purbeck stone. Defoe commented in the early eighteenth century that

the isle of Purbeck is eminent for vast quarrys of stone which is cut out flat, and us'd in London in great quantities for paving court-yards, alleys, avenues to houses, kitchens, footways on the sides of the high-streets, and the like; and is very profitable to the place, as also in the number of shipping employed in bringing it to London.

By the end of the eighteenth century it was estimated that 400 people were employed in the quarries and that 50,000 tons of stone were shipped from Swanage annually.

The stone from the island of Portland was comparatively little used during the middle ages, and extensive quarrying did not begin until the seventeenth century. The reason for this was that although the best Portland stone is of extremely high quality—the finest limestone in

England—it lies under some 30 ft of rubble or 'overburden', and it was not until the seventeenth century, when Inigo Jones popularised the stone by using it for the portico of the Banqueting Hall at Whitehall and for the reconstruction of old St Pauls, that there was sufficient demand or capital available to support the labour involved in large-scale quarrying. Leland, who wrote at length about Portland in the 1540s, and who obviously found the wild landscape of the island with its isolated and suspicious inhabitants very interesting, does not mention stone-quarrying there at all. In 1593 a survey of the royal manor of Portland reported that there were quarries in the cliffs which were let for five shillings per annum, but the surveyor was much more impressed by the oil-bearing shale which he found along the shore, 'a kinde of blacke stone or oare earth of Minerall matter apte to burne. . . .' By 1650, however, the quarries on the island were evidently important and were said to be worth £5 per annum. The really massive development of the Portland quarries occurred after 1666, when the stone was chosen by Wren for the construction of the new St Paul's and for the city churches after the Fire of London. Thereafter it rapidly became extremely popular and from the eighteenth century onwards Portland stone was used for churches and buildings all over the country, wherever it could conveniently be transported by sea, and great quantities of the stone were also exported. Stone-quarrying on the island of Portland continued up to the twentieth century to be a principal industrial activity of Dorset and one of the largest employers of labour. As quarrying expanded on the island during the eighteenth century the problem of getting the stone from the high central plateau down the steep slope to the piers along the coast became increasingly difficult. Several accounts exist of the remarkable way in which this was done. Perhaps the most dramatic description was written by the Rev. J. Skinner, the archaeologist and antiquarian vicar of Camerton near Bath, who visited the island in September 1804. He noted in his journal the following account of the method of hauling stone:

Large-hewn stones lie scattered in all directions; indeed the quarries worked on the Island are prodigious, and the mode of conveying the ponderous masses down the steep unavoidably arrests the attention of the stranger. The blocks being placed on a strong wooden carriage, with solid wheels appropriate to the weight they are to sustain, two horses are harnessed on before and one and sometimes two behind; the latter being supplied with strong breeching in order to act as drawbacks to the carriage, and prevent its running with too great velocity down the steep; indeed the sagacity and exertions of these poor animals in the arduous employment, is really astonishing; they squat down on their haunches, and suffer themselves to be dragged for many yards, struggling with all their strength against the weight that forces them forwards. To one unaccustomed to the sight, it appears as though their limbs must inevitably be dislocated, or their sinews cracked by the violence of their exertions: indeed one compassionates these poor creatures, the rather as all this labour might easily be obviated, by the simple construction of a railroad. Why this has not been long since performed is to me surprising, especially as Portland stone is in universal request.

In fact, it was not until 1826 that a tramway for conveying stone down the steep hillside to the piers was opened on the island.

Many quarrymen, both in Purbeck and Portland, combined their work with farming. The eighteenth-century historian of Dorset, John Hutchins, wrote of Portland that 'The corn of every sort is mostly cut down by the reap-hook, which the women use with great dexterity, and get in most of the harvest; for the men make such good wages in the quarries that they do not chose to leave the work.' In Purbeck many of the quarrymen were also farmers and the well-established tradition of combining the two occupations is to be seen very clearly in the probate inventories, or lists of all the goods and chattels of recently deceased people which had to be made in order to prove a will, and which survive for Corfe Castle, the main centre of the Purbeck stone quarries.

Other important stone quarries in the region included Ham Hill, where was extracted the lovely honey-coloured stone used in buildings over a wide area of south Somerset and north-west Dorset, and even farther afield; this is the stone of which both Sherborne Abbey and Montacute House are built, and it was also used for many of the great church towers of Somerset, several of which were built during the early years of the sixteenth century.

Notable also were the quarries on Mendip, at Doulting, Dundry, and elsewhere; and the quarries of Bath stone which acquired a great importance during the eighteenth century when they were exploited by Ralph Allen to provide building materials for the expansion of Bath itself as a fashionable spa, as well as for new houses and churches in Bristol and elsewhere. Much of the best Bath stone came from Hazelbury quarry near Box in Wiltshire, and it was this stone which was used during the middle ages for many of the churches and monasteries of the area, including Malmesbury, Stanley Abbey, Bradenstoke Priory, Lacock Abbey and Monkton Farleigh Priory. It was also used during the sixteenth century for Longleat House, and for many of the manor houses of north and west Wiltshire. In the south of Wiltshire the most important quarry was at Chilmark, and it was stone from Chilmark and from the nearby quarry at Teffont Evias which was used for Salisbury cathedral, and for many other churches and houses in that area including Wilton House.

The building of the Wilts. and Berks. canal and the Kennet and Avon canal, and later, the coming of the railways, gave a great impetus to the quarries of Wiltshire, and enabled stone from Box to be dispatched to London and all over the country. The search for Bath stone was extended below ground by mining, and created the great net-work of tunnels and underground workings which exist today around Corsham. During much of the nineteenth century the quarries and stone-mines were operated by a number of small companies, but in 1887 several of these amalgamated to form the Bath Stone Firms, a company which was later to become the Bath and Portland Stone Firms, and was to dominate stone-quarrying over the whole region.

Mining activity in the region was largely confined to the Mendip area and north Somerset, and was concerned with the extraction of lead and coal. Lead had been mined on Mendip since the Roman period, and the industry continued to be important down to the middle of the nineteenth century, though it reached its peak during the sixteenth and seventeenth centuries, when production expanded very rapidly under the impetus of improved organisation and new technical skills. The lead-mining part of Mendip was divided into four Liberties—Charterhouse, Harptree, St Cuthberts (Priddy) and Chewton. Within these liberties mining was closely controlled by a complicated structure of ancient laws and customs which regulated all mining work.

The lead-mining industry declined steadily after about 1700, due to the exhaustion of the more easily accessible veins, difficulties with flooding, lack of investment in new machinery, and, above all, competition from cheaper lead from elsewhere. The industry had a brief revival during the nineteenth century when the slag which had been left by earlier smelters was re-smelted, using new and improved techniques. But this also had declined by the end of the nineteenth century with the exhaustion of the available slag.

Coal-mining also had a long history on the northern fringe of Mendip and in north Somerset, in the Radstock—Midsomer Norton area and around Bishops Sutton, Pensford, Clutton, Queen Charlton, Brislington, Kilmersdon and Camerton, and at Nailsea. Like the lead-miners, workers in the coal industry commonly combined mining and farming, although with the expansion of coal-mining during the eighteenth and nineteenth centuries the region saw the development of several villages and small towns which were almost totally dependent upon mining, and the growth of housing and social conditions which will be discussed in Chapter 4. The coal industry declined rapidly during the twentieth century, and now, like lead-mining, it has ceased to exist in the region.

In addition to the major rural industries, there have always existed throughout the region a host of minor industries, many of them confined to particular small areas and supplying part-time work to the farming population, thereby playing a very important part in the economic life of the community. Such traditional industries include tanning which was found widely, particularly throughout the cattle-raising, clayland areas; gloving; and fishing along the Dorset and Somerset coasts. The latter was frequently combined with either farming or with some other activity such as for example stone-quarrying in Purbeck and Portland or cloth, rope or sailcloth working around Bridport and Lyme Regis. The manufacture of gloves was carried on very widely throughout the region, though its main centre was at Yeovil. Since this was mainly a home industry it has left few records, but the numerous references to glovers and to the sale of gloves, especially in Yeovil and south Somerset, from the sixteenth century onwards, leaves no doubt of its importance. The village of Stoke-sub-Hamdon which lies under Ham Hill in south Somerset was also an important centre of the gloving industry, especially during the nineteenth century when the population increased rapidly through newcomers encouraged to settle there because of the growth of the industry. Much of the work was done by people in their own homes as a spare-time occupation, and particularly by women, but by 1844 there were four glove factories established at Stoke, producing silk, cotton and tafetta gloves as well as the more regular leather gloves. Glove-making was also carried on in various parts of Wiltshire and provided an important by-employment.

Paper-making was also a widespread craft in the region from the sixteenth century onwards wherever there was a local demand and the essential adequate supply of pure water. Paper-mills were to be found throughout the Hampshire, Wiltshire and Dorset chalkland areas, where there were unlimited supplies of clear water from the chalk streams, and in Somerset where the Mendip streams were extremely well suited to paper-making. Other rural crafts included brewing and cider-making; the making of hurdles, rakes and other articles from hazel spars, a craft which was to be found all over the chalklands where the sheep-folds used vast quantities of hurdles; the making of baskets and wickerwork goods from the withies grown in the Somerset levels; clay extraction and tobacco-pipe making on the Dorset heathland and in parts of Wiltshire—John Aubrey wrote that 'The best (pipes) for shape and colour . . . are made at Amesbury . . . .

They may be called chimneys portable in pockets, the one end being the hearth and the other the tunnel thereof.' Employment for women and girls in various parts of the region was also provided by straw-bonnet making, lace and stay making, stocking knitting and by 'buttony' or the construction of very elaborate fancy buttons, a craft centred particularly on the Blandford and Sturminster Newton area of Dorset. Finally there were in all the villages of the region a number of the more usual craftsmen, the blacksmiths, carpenters, bakers, boot and shoe makers, thatchers, builders, etc., many of whom also combined their crafts with farming or some other activity. Some indication of the range of crafts to be found even in a small village throughout the whole of this period, which made the inhabitants self-sufficient in most of their daily wants, may be seen for example in the village of Yetminster, in north Dorset, where in 1848 there were nearly 20 different crafts and trades, including a saddler, several boot- and shoe-makers, a glazier, miller, maltster, tailor, carpenters, blacksmiths, thatchers and carriers. In a little market town such as Cranborne at the same time 25 different trades were being carried on, and the town population of some 2,500 included brick-layers, plasterers, a straw-bonnet maker, a plumber, cooper, wheelwrights and two smiths as well as several shop-keepers. In Somerset, the village of Pensford in the north of the county, which was distinguished from the neighbouring villages only by the existence of a small weekly market, had in 1830 five inns, several shops, a baker, tailor, miller, butcher, blacksmiths, carpenters, shoemakers, a cooper, farrier, saddler, wheelwright, and a painter, as well as various carriers and general dealers. It was this self-sufficiency of the rural communities, which could meet almost all the day-to-day needs of the inhabitants, that provided the secure basis for the strong community life which characterised them.

4. Domestic life

In considering the daily lives of people living in the Wessex region at any time during the years from 1500 to 1900, it is important constantly to bear in mind the very great differences which existed between the various classes of society throughout the whole period. These four centuries saw profound changes in all aspects of rural life, yet the dominant characteristic of society was still in 1900 as it had been in 1500 the great disparity between rich and poor in the conditions of their everyday existence. There was little comparison between the harsh conditions in which most labourers lived throughout the whole period and the affluence and luxury of the richer gentry, insulated by their wealth from many of the difficulties which daily afflicted their less prosperous neighbours. This is still apparent to the most casual visitor to the region from the number, size and splendour of the great houses with which the area is so abundantly endowed, or from the opulence and magnificence of the memorials left by the wealthy families, both in the form of monuments in churches and cathedrals and in the landscapes, parks and gardens which they created. It is clear that the life of the fortunate inhabitants of such places as, for example, Dunster, Melbury, Wimborne St Giles, Hinton St George, Longleat, Lydiard Tregoze or of a host of other country houses, large and small, was very far removed even from that of the farmers and tradesmen of the region, and was in a quite different world from the daily conditions of the poorer craftsmen, smallholders or labourers. The daily life of the household in the houses of the gentry families of the region throughout the period can be seen very clearly from the wealth of surviving documentary evidence— account books, inventories, surveys, etc., as well as detailed descriptions. For example, the first Lord Shaftesbury of Wimborne St Giles left a vivid description of the manor house of one of his neighbours, a typical country gentleman, Henry Hastings, the squire of Woodland in east Dorset during the early seventeenth century. The house was situated in a large park, well-stocked with deer, and the principal ground-floor rooms consisted of a great hall with a parlour beyond and a separate kitchen and domestic offices. The hall was the living-room for the whole household, and was

strewed with marrow bones, full of hawks perches, hounds, spaniels and terriers, the upper sides of the hall hung with foxskins of this and the last year's skinning, here and there a polecat intermixed, guns and keepers' and huntsmens' poles in abundance. The parlour was a large long room, as properly furnished; on a great hearth paved with brick lay some terriers and the choicest hounds and spaniels; seldom but two of the great chairs had litters of young cats in them, which were not to be disturbed, he (Henry Hastings) having always three and four attending him at dinner, and a little white round stick of fourteen inches long lying by his trencher, that he might defend such meat as he had no mind to part with to them . . . .

Evidence of the style of life and household expenses of one of the wealthiest and most notable of all the families of the region is to be found in the family papers of the Cecils, Earls of Salisbury, who, besides their great palace at Hatfield also acquired early in the seventeenth century the manor house at Cranborne and much of the land in the surrounding area. Vast sums were spent on the house and gardens at Cranborne by Robert Cecil the First Earl of Salisbury, and some indication of the personal expenditure and the manner in which he lived is shown in the expenses he incurred on a visit to Cranborne in March 1613. The journey from London by coach took three days and included such items as 'To a carter on Windsor Heath that helped the coach being fast 12d' as well as sums to almhouses along the route and to musicians who played to the Earl at each stop. One night was spent at Salisbury where 20 shillings was distributed to the poor of the town, 20 shillings to the musicians, 20 shillings 'to the ringers that rang at my lords coming to the town' and two shillings 'to the beadle that kept the poor in order from troubling my Lord.' At Cranborne lavish payments were made for provisions which included capons, brawn, lambs, pheasants, partridges, turkeys, woodcocks, pike, salmon, carp and cheeses; further payments for the hounds and huntsmen when my lord went hunting; great expense when the whole party went to Salisbury for a day at the races including coloured ribbons for all the guests and retainers, drummers, trumpeters and musketeers. The whole visit lasted only ten days, but the total cost came to £276 0s 11d. Similar lavish expenditure was incurred by Lord Salisbury at Cranborne in August 1618 when King James I was entertained there. The total cost of entertaining the royal party amounted to £405 19s 0d, and included the following provisions for the royal banquet:

3 bullocks
48 sheep
20 calves
33 lambs
38 tongues
43 udders
56 marrow bones
5 deer's tongues

as well as poultry and fish sent from London including ducks, capons, turkeys, pheasants, herons, curlews, larks, partridges, chickens, etc., and fish of all sorts. The wine purchased for the occasion included 250 gallons of claret, 28 gallons of sack, 14 gallons of Rhenish wine, 27 gallons of white wine and 1,750 gallons of beer.

The kitchen book of the Poulett family for the great house at Hinton St George survives for parts of the seventeenth and eighteenth centuries, and shows regular, lavish expenditure on provisions and drink for the household. During May 1697, for example, besides the ordinary purchases, the cook bought soles, plaice, lobsters, crabs and quantities of other, unspecified fish, pigeons, pigeons' eggs, cowslips, laver, 'hartichoakes', sugar, nutmegs, pepper and lemons. Similar details of lavish expenditure on the regular running of a great household from the sixteenth to the nineteenth centuries can be seen, for example, in the papers of the Lutterells of Dunster Castle, the Herberts of Wilton, the Welds of Lulworth Castle and a host of others, and on a rather less extravagant but nonetheless affluent scale in the account books of a host of lesser families in manor houses all over the region.

During the nineteenth century, for example, an indoor staff of 27 was kept by the Earl of Shaftesbury at Wimborne St Giles, as well as an army of men employed in the gardens and stables. The Poulett's indoor staff at Hinton St George included a steward, butler, housekeeper, cook and footmen, as well as a dozen maids employed in various capacities, all in a carefully regulated hierarchy and kept under a remarkably strict regime. The sort of discipline under which the servants in a large household lived is seen in the butler's book belonging to the Hippisley estate at Ston Easton in north Somerset. This gives in detail the regulations for the servants, the times of their meals, and the general rules for the conduct of the household. For example, men servants were allowed a pint of beer each with their dinners, maidservants two-thirds of a pint each; 'If unnecessarily unpunctual or unclean they are to go without any thing until the next meal.' Household servants often came from the same families over many generations. Notable in this respect was the Stillingfleet family who served the Earls of Salisbury at Cranborne as housekeepers, stewards and household servants in an uninterrupted succession from the seventeenth to the nineteenth centuries. Further evidence of the sense of family pride, ostentation, grandeur and leadership of county society among the gentry families of the region, is to be seen in the sumptuous monuments which they have left in scores of country churches. Monuments like, for example, those of the St Johns and Mompessons at Lydiard Tregoze, the Newtons at Yatton and East Harptree, the Horseys and Digbys at Sherborne or the Wroughtons and Glanvilles at Broad Hinton, show, perhaps more clearly than anything else, the pride, wealth and unselfconscious acceptance of superiority of these and similar families, which continued to dominate rural society throughout the period. Such families were far removed in wealth and style of life from even the richest farmers on their estates, and they effectively lived in a different world from that inhabited by most other members of rural society.

YEOMEN AND HUSBANDMEN

Much detail about the possessions and life-style of the working farmers of the region during the sixteenth and seventeenth centuries can be reconstructed from their probate inventories, or lists of their goods and chattels which were made after their death for the purpose of proving their wills in the church courts. During the sixteenth and seventeenth centuries most farmers had comparatively few possessions in their houses; most of their wealth was tied up in their farm stock, crops and equipment, and few farmers, even those with a total wealth well above the average, possessed clothing valued at more than £5. Their houses, too, were remarkably sparsely furnished, particularly compared to the mass of furniture commonly to be found in Victorian farmhouses. Because of the way in which farming varied so greatly in different parts of the region, it is difficult to choose 'typical' examples to illustrate the household goods and possessions of the 'average' yeoman and husbandman, but a fairly well-to-do farmer in the region during the seventeenth century would have had no more than 20 per cent of his total wealth in his household furnishings and personal possessions. An example of the sort of household goods possessed by a small farmer of well below average wealth is seen in the probate inventory of William Graynger who farmed at Calne in Wiltshire and who died in April 1597. His total wealth amounted to only £13 6s 0d, most of which was in his three cows and his butter and cheese-making equipment. He also made part of his living from weaving and possessed a spinning-wheel and a loom. His house consisted of two rooms, and in the hall he had a table, a form, a chair and a cupboard; while before the open fire was a pair of pothooks, a frying pan, a pottinger and a skillet. He also possessed 'Three brass potts, fyve pewter platters, 5 pottingers, 8 sawcers, five salte cellars, 2 pewter cups, 2 pewter candelsticks and one brazen chaffing dish.' In the bedchamber he had one bedstead, with a mattress, canvas sheets, blankets and coverlet, two coffers, one rack for storing his cheese, a lantern and a basket. This, together with his few clothes, made up his entire personal wealth.

Rather higher up the social scale was John Elford of Chetnole in the parish of Yetminster in north Dorset who is described as 'Yeoman' and who died in March 1637 worth £101 13s 8d, an above-average figure for a working farmer at this time. He also evidently depended for his income mainly on his cows and on the sale of butter and cheese, but he also had a by-employment as a candlemaker. His house consisted of a hall, kitchen, buttery and shop on the ground floor with two chambers above. Most of his wealth was accounted for by his eight cows, eight calves and three bullocks and by the tallow and candles in his workshop. But in his hall he had a long table with one form, five stools and a chair, one cupboard containing various pewter cups and plates, and, before the fire, one spit, a pair of pothooks, and a pair of tongs. He also had two brass candlesticks and 'one playning iron and a pair of Bellowes.' The kitchen contained 'a payre of scales and beames, with weight stones and a chopping knife' as well as various pieces of cooking equipment. In the buttery he kept his cheese- and butter-making utensils and 2 cwt of cheese, while the shop contained tallow and candles, soap, wicks and moulds for candles. The two bedrooms contained between them three bedsteads with all their sheets, pillows, blankets and coverlets. This with his clothing completed the list of all the possessions of this man, who was among the richer of his fellow farmer/craftsmen in north Dorset at this time.

During the course of the seventeenth century the standard of living and the amount of the personal possessions of the more affluent farmers mounted steadily as did the size and quality of their houses, but the poorer labourers remained miserably poor and with very few belongings.

LABOURERS

While there are many records, including the highly informative probate inventories, which provide information about the wealthier farmers and the prosperous yeomen of the sixteenth and seventeenth centuries, there are far fewer sources relating to the domestic life of the smallholders and day-labourers. Some wills and inventories survive to show the few posses-sions which they owned, but many did not leave such documents and those with goods worth less than £5 were not in any case obliged to do so. It is clear that their houses were very sparsely furnished indeed, and must have been very uncomfortable, especially in winter; it is also apparent that their cooking facilities were of the most rudimentary kind and could have provided only the plainest of diet. Their clothing varied with the type of farm work upon which they were engaged: shepherds and herds-men wore long warm cloaks made of the heavy west of England cloth, a perquisite of their jobs which was generally provided by their employers. John Aubrey described the seventeenth-century dress of the shepherds on Salisbury Plain as 'a long white cloake with a very deep cape which comes halfway down their backs, made of the locks of the sheep.' Carters and ploughmen wore smocks made of woollen cloth, linen or canvas, while general farm labourers wore baggy breeches, woollen stockings, a cloth shirt and jerkin or cloak. The manufacture of straw and felt hats and the knitting of heavy woollen stockings provided an important by-employ-ment in many parts of the region. Clothing made of west of England cloth was not only very warm, but also extremely hard-wearing and could be handed on from one person to another, often no doubt with somewhat ill-fitting results. Footwear consisted of heavy leather boots or shoes, some-times double-soled for additional waterproofing, and made of locally produced oak-bark tanned leather. The clothing of the wives and daughters of small farmers and labourers remained generally plain and simple until the nineteenth century, and contemporary records seldom contain any mention of other articles of female attire for the poorer classes than a dress or gown, a petticoat or shift, together with an apron and a straw hat. Women also wore pattens or overshoes as some protection against mud and mire; notices exhorting the wearers of pattens to take them off before entering church can still be seen in some church porches, for example at Trent on the borders of Somerset and Dorset, or at Hawkesbury, over the Wiltshire border in Gloucestershire.

Records concerning the apprenticing of pauper children often provide evidence of the sort of clothing which was considered suitable for them, since the overseers of the poor commonly provided a complete new outfit for the young apprentices. Thus when a young boy, Thomas Stevens, was sent by the overseers of the poor at Yetminster to be apprenticed to a shoemaker at Exeter in 1675, they provided him with a coat, waistcoat and breeches made of woollen cloth, a hat, pair of shoes, and a linen shift and neck cloth. And Elizabeth Sprackler of Crewkerne in

1750 was given a gown made of 'linsey-woolsey' which was a mixture of linen and wool, and petticoat, a pair of shoes and stockings and a hat.

Farm labourers living in their masters' houses undoubtedly enjoyed a much higher standard of living than did most of those who had their own cottages. Often the larger farms provided lodgings for farm servants in a loft or over the stables or cowhouse, an arrangement which had the advantage of providing additional warmth for the occupants during the winter. There are several seventeenth-century references to lodging rooms and houses for servants on demesne farms in various parts of Wiltshire, for example at Broadchalke and Amesbury, and the inmates of such lodging houses would commonly have had their meals with the farmer and his family. Many labourers' cottages throughout the whole of the period 1500–1900 were no more than hovels of cob and thatch, often erected on some piece of waste ground or isolated part of the common, and put up overnight in the belief that such a rapid construction gave squatters' rights to the inhabitants; and the furnishings of these cabins were as rudimentary as their structure. An example of the way in which such labourers' flimsy cottages could be set up is to be seen in the court rolls of the manor of Cranborne, where in 1625 some of the tenants complained to the Earl of Salisbury's steward there that a poor labourer, one Richard Cooke 'intends either this night or the next to set up a house (which he hath already framed) upon the common of Alderholt, and hath placed straw upon the common in the place he hath made choyce of to erect his house in . . . .' In this instance the tenants objected because they claimed that the number of squatters who were already established on the common was so great that the common grazing-land available for their cattle was severely restricted, and they wished stop any further encroachments. There are many other examples of the establishment of such squatters' settlements. A survey of Kingston Lacy made in 1591 listed 30 cottages recently built on the waste and heathland there; and in 1598 the Commissioners of the Duchy of Lancaster complained that one Thomas Chater had enclosed an acre of the heath at Holt Forest and had erected a cottage there 'at a place called Crooked Wythes . . . which is verie inconvenient, as well for the spoyling of the deere as for the spoyling of the woods and otherwise.' In spite of these complaints the cottage survived and still stands today in its acre enclosure at Crooked Withies. It must have been substantially built from the outset; others were much more flimsy in their construction. At Fordington in the early seventeenth century there were said to be many newly erected cottages but 'these poore houses being erected onlie for ye shelter of poore people . . . are not much to be valued.' Similarly at Netherbury in 1626 a complaint was made to the Quarter Sessions that

there are now Latelie erected eight or ten poor Cottages on which divers poore people dwell, and it being farre from the rest of the Tythinge where usuallie the Tythingeman dwelleth, they take libertie to themselves to keepe unlicensed alehouses and have diverse disorderlie meetings where (it is feared) manie stollen goods are consumed to the greate griefe and losse of many honest neighbours. . . .

Newcomers, sub-tenants and squatters were generally unpopular with established residents who resented the depletion of the natural resources, and they were regarded with the greatest suspicion by the overseers of the poor, who naturally feared that they would become a charge upon the parish rates. Nevertheless the problem of squatters' settlements and of unauthorised cottages continued throughout the seventeenth and eighteenth centuries, and the increase in population served to exacerbate the problems of both employment and housing. The noted surveyor John Norden found a situation at Cerne Abbas in 1617 which illustrates the problem faced by many villages and market towns. He wrote that

. . . they that injoye the principall howses of the towne dwell from them and lett them to a masse of base people, meere mendicantes. As namelie one Mr John Nobley hath a fayer howse but noe competent under tenant. Mr Lovelace also hath a fayre howse full of poore people. One Mr Fowell, Mr Devenishe and one John Williams, which laste hath a fayer howse and hath put neer a dozen lowsy people in it . . . .

Shortage of housing in some parts of the region, coupled with the unwillingness of many parishes to accept newcomers, meant that some unfortunate people were reduced to desperate circumstances, and were either compelled to seek shelter in the parish poor-house or some hovel, or alternatively to risk the very severe laws against unlicensed wanderers and beggars and take to the road.

In 1610 Lacock was said to be 'surcharged by the multitude of inmates and those of the poorest sort to the number of sixtie persons like to lye in the Streete for want of houses . . .'; and in 1647 John Bevin and his wife of Brokenborough near Malmesbury, who had been evicted from the the house which they had rented, were 'constrained to dwell in a hollow tree in the streete . . . to the great hazard of their lives they being anncient people.'

The squatters who erected their cottages and hovels on uncultivated wastes and commons had little or no legal right to the land they appropriated, and over most of the chalklands, where manorial control was much stricter, squatters were generally prevented from settling. But in the clay-lands and heaths where tracts of common or ancient woodland remained, many such communities came into existence; the inhabitants making their living by day labour in agriculture or industry, and gradually acquiring a right to their cottages only because manorial authorities, either through negligence or because they needed the labour, turned a blind eye to their existence. A good example of such a squatters' community grew up on the waste-land at the edge of Warminster Common in Wiltshire, in an area of heath and woodland well away from the town. During the seventeenth century a few small cottages were built there, and in spite of half-hearted attempts by the Longleat estate to prevent the growth of the settlement, other squatters' hovels were erected during the eighteenth century. By 1781 there were more than 1,000 people living there in some 200 cottages and hovels, most of them consisting of no more than one room up and one down, with earth floors, no ceilings, and lacking even the barest facilities. The water-supply came from the stream which was polluted with filth and rubbish, disease was rampant there, and the place was notorious for violence, crime and drunkenness.

HOUSING AND DIET
The development of the great houses of the wealthy section of society is already well known and carefully documented. The medieval tradition of a great hall, often open to the roof, with a services wing containing kitchen and pantry etc., at one end, and a private wing with bedrooms and parlour at the other, gave way during the sixteenth and seventeenth centuries to a desire for greater comfort and privacy, and the great hall as the central feature of the house disappeared in favour of a multiplicity of rooms used for different purposes. At the same time the fashion of the time demanded a symmetrical front to the whole building, a development which was to continue through the eighteenth century. For the much more numerous though less impressive houses and cottages of the mass of the population, building styles and methods changed little through the six-teenth and seventeenth centuries, and close dating of these houses is often very difficult or impossible. Until the coming of the railways, the building materials were all obtained locally, and varied greatly across the region—ashlar, stone, rubble, flint, chalk, cob, timber and brick—each within fairly clearly defined geographical limits according to the local availability of supplies. Roofing-material also varied from thatch of straw or reed to slate and stone tiles. The plans and arrangement of rooms within the smaller houses were equally diverse, although certain basic plans are recognisable.

During the sixteenth and seventeenth centuries the most common arrangement for farmhouses and for larger cottages, especially in areas where building stone was available, was a range of three ground-floor rooms, with a through passage between two of them and a central chimney heating the innermost room. This central room was the main living-room of the house, while one unheated room was the parlour, still often used for sleeping-quarters, and the other was the kitchen and storeroom. Smaller houses frequently had two ground-floor rooms of unequal size, the larger having the fireplace and chimney which was accommodated in an end wall. Many examples of both these types survive throughout the region. The eighteenth century saw the introduction of more chimneys for heating two or more rooms, and of double-depth arrangement of rooms, together with the beginnings of symmetrical front elevations, similar to those being introduced in the houses of the wealthy. Smaller houses and labourers' cottages of the nineteenth century show less variety of plan, except in those places where estate houses were built to the designs of a particular land-owner or his architect. With the coming of the railways, materials became much more standardised as cheap brick, tiles and other articles began moer and more to replace the traditional regional supplies.

It is evident from the surviving household account-books that the richer families could afford the luxury of a varied diet by the addition of imported or expensive items such as oranges, lemons, nutmegs and other spices, as well as fish, game and various kinds of meat and wine. But the food of the smallholders and labourers of the region was generally poor and monotonous throughout the whole period. Bread was their main standby, and was generally made entirely of wheat in the Wessex region, unlike some other parts of the country less well suited for corn growing. Cheese, bacon, vegetables and soup made from peas and beans made up the other mainstays of the diet of the poorer classes. Preparation of all but the simplest meals presented a great problem for most housewives, since labourers' cottages lacked adequate cooking facilities, and, in particular, few had ovens. Over much of the chalklands, where trees were scarce, it was also difficult to obtain sufficient fuel, and manorial regulations often prohibited the use of private ovens because of the great risk of fire in the compact, thatch-roofed villages of the chalkland valleys. In some manors a common bakehouse was provided for the use of the tenants, and the court rolls of many manors, mostly on the chalklands, contain injunctions that tenants should use only the common manorial bakehouse. Most of the food eaten by labourers and their families had therefore of necessity to be either cooked before an open fire, or to be boiled or fried. Beer was the main drink

1

2

3

4

6

7

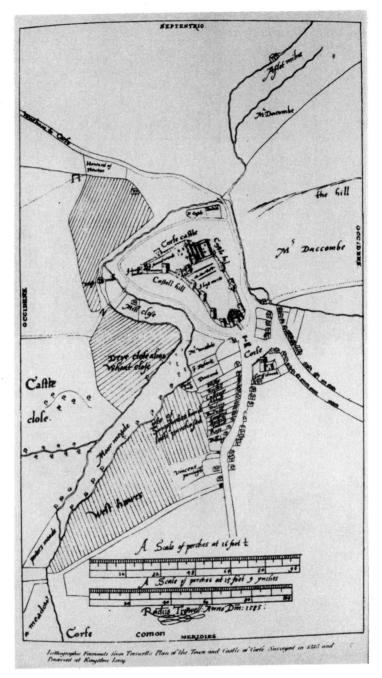

SEPTENTRIO

Aftei milne

Mᵗ Daccombe

the hill

Mˢ Daccombe

Corfe caftle

Castell hill

Hill clofe

Dry clofe alias Wheat clofe

Corfe

Caftle clofe.

Floor meade

Weft hawes

A Scale of perches at 16 foot ½

16   32   48   64   80   96

A Scale of perches at 15 foot 9 ynches

Radus Treswell Anno Dm: 1585:

meadow

Corfe   comon

MERIDIES

Lithographic facsimile from Treswell's Plan of the Town and Castle of Corfe Surveyed in 1585 and Preserved at Kingston Lacy.

8

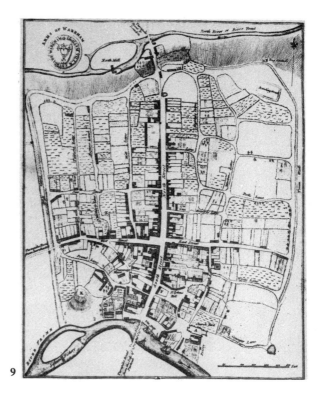

9

10

11

12

13

14

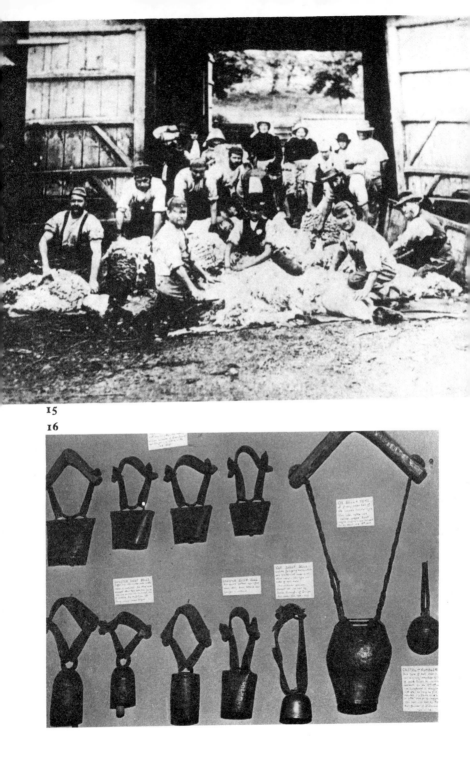

15

16

A
TREATISE

ON

WATERING MEADOWS.

WHEREIN

ARE SHEWN SOME OF THE MANY ADVAN-
TAGES ARISING FROM THAT

MODE of PRACTICE,

PARTICULARLY ON

COARSE, BOGGY, or BARREN LANDS.

With Four COPPER PLATES.

Flooding is truly the beft of all Improvements,
where it can be effected : and there ought not to be
a fingle Acre of Land neglected, which is capable
of it.   KENT's Hints to the Landed Intereft.

Affiduity, Experience and Common Senfe form a far
furer Guide to us, than Fancy and Theory.
ANONYMOUS.

19

20

21

22

23

24

25

BLANDFORD
AGRICULTURAL SOCIETY,
ESTABLISHED 1839,
FOR THE ENCOURAGEMENT OF INDUSTRIOUS LABOURERS AND SERVANTS.

CERTIFICATE OF MERIT.

No. _39_   Class _1_

This is to Certify, that on the _20th_ Day of _December_ 18_56_ a Premium of _a Coat & 10s_ was awarded by the COMMITTEE of the Blandford Agricultural Society to _George Giles_ _Servant to Mr George Hill for having worked 30 years on the same farm & always maintained a good character_ _Given by the Rt Hon George Banks MP_

As Witness our Hands, _J J Farquharson_ President
James Burgess
Mr C Matthews } Members of the
Henry Foakes } Committee.

28

30
→

29

31

32

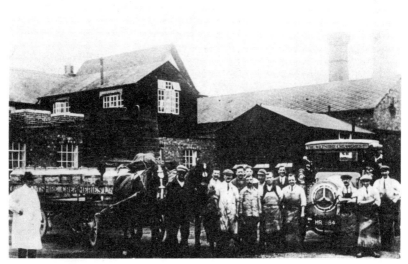

34

35

36

37

High Street, Marlborough

38

39

40

41

42

43

44

45

46

47

Castle Combe Association,

FOR

THE PREVENTION

OF

ROBBERIES AND THEFTS,

AND FOR THE

PROTECTION of PERSONS and PROPERTY.

THE FOLLOWING REWARDS,

INDEPENDANT OF THOSE ALLOWED BY ACT OF PARLIAMENT,

Are to be paid to any Person (not being a Member of this Society) who shall give Information, upon Oath, of the Person or Persons guilty of any of the respective Offences following, committed on the Persons or Property of any of the Members of this Society, one half of such Reward to be paid on Commitment of the Offender, or Offenders, (if any Commitment shall take place,) and the remainder (or the whole in case of no previous Commitment,) on his, her, or their Conviction:

	£.	s.	d.
Murder, Burglary, Housebreaking, Shoplifting, Highway-Robbery, or setting Fire to any Dwelling-House, Barn, or other Out-house, or to any Mow or Stack of Corn, Grain, Hay, Wood, or Fuel	5	5	0
Stealing, or wilfully and Feloniously killing or maiming any Horse, Mare, Gelding, Ox, Bull, Cow, Calf, or Sheep	5	5	0
Stealing any Waggon, Cart, Plough, or other Implement in Husbandry, or any Hay, Seed, Corn, or Grain threshed or unthreshed	2	2	0
Stealing Pigs or Poultry	1	1	0
Buying or receiving Stolen Goods, knowing the same to have been Stolen	2	2	0
Cutting, Breaking down, Lopping, Topping, Burning, or damaging any Timber, Trees, or Stealing or breaking any Gates, Bars, Hurdles, Hedges, Pales, Rails, Posts, Iron-work, Gardening Tools, or Implements in any Trade or Business; or Stealing, Pulling up or destroying Turnips, or other Roots or Vegetables, in any Field, Garden, Orchard, or other Place	0	10	6
For Information of any other Offence, amounting to Larceny, not hereinbefore particularized	0	10	6

No Compromise with Offenders is allowed on any pretence whatsoever, and Persons guilty of such Offence are to be prosecuted at the Expence of this Society.

MEMBERS:

CASTLE COMBE.

The Hon. T. R. ARUNDELL
WILLIAM SCROPE, Esq.
Mr. FRANCIS CHILD
Mr. ELVER NEWMAN
Mr. SAMUEL CHAPPELL
Mr. WILLIAM BEAK, Jun.
Mr. THOMAS SEALY
Mr. GEORGE DAWSON

Mrs. ANN SARGENT
Mr. RICHARD SARGENT
Mr. JAMES DREW

GRITTLETON.

Mr. GEORGE TOGHILL
Mr. WILLIAM SEALY

NETTLETON.

Rev. D. R. GODFREY

Mr. WILLIAM COATES
Mr. JAMES TAYLER

WEST KINGTON.

Rev. J. J. HUME
Mr. JOSEPH KING

YATTON-KEYNEL.

Rev. THOMAS HOOPER
Mr. JAMES HOLLOWAY.

☞ *A General Meeting to be held at the* SALUTATION FOSS HOUSE, *in the Parish of Castle Combe, on the last Thursday in October in every Year.*

BAILY, PRINTER, CALNE.

49

50

throughout the corn-growing chalklands, but in the claylands, where good malting barley was less easily produced, it was cider which provided the staple beverage. As will be shown later, very large quantities of beer and cider were consumed, especially at harvest-time. It was perhaps the tedium and harshness of everyday life in these rural communities, as well as the monotony of diet, which led men to seek an escape through the alehouse, and it is clear from a variety of contemporary sources that there was an amazing amount of drunkenness, particularly during the sixteenth and seventeenth centuries. By far the commonest entries in the records both of Quarter Sessions and of individual justices are those concerned with unlicensed tippling houses, excessive drinking, drunkenness, unlawful gaming at alehouses and other connected offences. In all the counties of the region before the eighteenth century these problems even out-number the entries on bastardy or the care of paupers. Even church functions were not exempt from drunkenness, and in Somerest in 1628, for example, there was a public warning against the disorders and excessive drinking associated with 'the keeping of publique Revells, Church Ales, Clerks Ales and other Ales.'

Churchwardens' presentments were also full of reports of drunkenness, tippling during the time of divine service, excessive numbers of alehouses, and even of brawling and disorder in church, as for example at Alton Pancras in 1617 where Henry Spinter was stated by the churchwardens to have been drunk in church and that

one Saboth daye a littell before the eveninge prayer went up into the tower and at a trappe dore did pisse downe upon theare heads in the belfry that they could not stand there nor neare itt to the great offence of those that were present . . . .

FIRES

The process of malting and brewing was one of the causes of many of the destructive fires which so frequently ravaged the towns and villages of the region. Several towns suffered repeated fires; for example, Beaminster was almost destroyed in 1644, but there had been several earlier fires there, and there were further major ones in 1684, 1781, 1786 and 1842, apart from a multitude of smaller ones confined to one or two houses. The great fire which so severely damaged Blandford Forum in 1731 was only the most serious in a whole series of conflagrations there, including major fires in 1579 and 1677. The long street of Marlborough was burnt to the ground in the space of five hours in 1653 when a strong wind fanned the flames, and the town suffered from further fires during the next century. The speed with which a fire could take hold and the amount of the destruction it could cause in a short time, together with the comparative powerlessness of contemporary fire-fighting equipment, made it one of the most dreaded features of life, particularly in the thatched-roof villages of the Wessex region. But in spite of the ever-present danger of fire in the tightly packed, timbered and thatched houses, people were surprisingly careless about the risks. Manorial and local government records contain constant exhortations about the perils of fire, and many examples of the hazards to which communities were exposed. Elaborate precautions were taken to try to ensure that chimneys were adequate, that hay- and corn-ricks were situated well away from kitchens, that common ovens, bakeries, smithies, malt-houses and breweries did not constitute a danger, but in spite of all efforts accidents still occurred. For example, in 1629 the Dorset justices were told of the widow Gaye who lived 'in the heart and middle of the towne of Wimborne Minster and who, though unlicensed, brewed great quantities of beer and ale 'in a Flew or chimney made of timber to the great danger of the whole towne.' They were told that the house had already caught fire once and was 'very likely to have adventured the whole towne.' And the Wiltshire justices in 1624 received a petition from the inhabitants of Wylye stating that one John Taylor

doth use the trade of bruing and baking in a house very unfit by reason it hath in it neyther Chymney nor flewe nor stone wale about it above the heigth of foure foot being a thetched house, without a loft and hath ben already once or twice like to set the towne on fire . . . .

The Wiltshire justices also dealt with the case of Jane Slye of Corton near Heytesbury, who in 1630 was said to be 'a verie careless woman in and about the carryeng and using her fier and candle in her barne, stables and cowhouse without any lantorne or any other good defence.' The parish records throughout the region are also full of the pathetic stories of those unfortunate families who had 'lost all by fire.'

EIGHTEENTH- AND NINETEENTH-CENTURY CONDITIONS

Conditions for farm labourers and their families did not improve during the eighteenth and nineteenth centuries, and in some ways were much worse in the nineteenth century than they had been in the sixteenth. Many of the traditional handicrafts and by-employments—spinning, stocking-knitting, the manufacture of lace, buttons, small tools and domestic articles, hat- and bonnet-making, and many others—which had provided an important additional income for farmers, labourers and their families, disappeared in the face of competition from cheap mass-produced articles.

The 'engrossing' or throwing together of smallholdings to make larger, more economic and profitable farms, with the accompanying eviction of the tenants of the former smallholdings and the disappearance of common lands in the face of enclosures, deprived many labourers of the small plots of land or the grazing-rights which had previously given them a subsidiary income as well as a certain measure of independence. Farm wages remained low in the region and during the eighteenth and nineteenth centuries (especially in Dorset) they were a by-word throughout the whole country; and although some of the great estates did much to try to improve their labourers' cottages, conditions in many places remained appalling. The various severe depressions in agriculture which occurred at the ending of the Napoleonic Wars, at various times during the 1830s and 1840s, and during the last decades of the century, led to unparalleled poverty, misery and degradation for some of the farm labourers and their families. It is very difficult to view these conditions in perspective and to strike the right balance between the abundant but often contradictory evidence which survives about rural conditions, for the miserable conditions of many farm labourers existed side by side with considerable wealth and affluence, particularly in the mid-nineteenth century, and it is clear that not all labourers and small farmers were affected by the grinding poverty which so many observers commented upon. The great number of solid well-built farm-houses and cottages as well as farm buildings dating from the nineteenth century, which are to be seen in almost every village throughout the region, show that there were sections even of the less wealthy classes in rural society who were enjoying a reasonable prosperity. Moreover the coming of the railways provided a possible escape-route for those who could seize the opportunity or who had the initiative to take it. Nonetheless, the evidence for the widespread poverty and distress and for the miserable conditions of domestic life of the poor which were caused by low wages, lack of employment, recurrent depressions in agriculture, the decline of the cloth-trade and other traditional by-employments, is abundant.

From the end of the eighteenth century ample evidence is available concerning the conditions of rural life; in particular, the nineteenth century saw a stream of accounts and statistics which were carefully compiled by various observers for the benefit of the multitude of Parliamentary commissions appointed to enquire into all aspects of rural life, agriculture, employment, education, poverty, housing and a host of other matters. This wealth of evidence, however, brings its own problems; it is necessary to beware of painting too black a picture or of concentrating too exclusively upon the extremes within society. The point made at the onset must be emphasised, that the opulence, extravagance and ostentation of the life of the great houses, with their multitude of servants, gamekeepers, horses and hounds, and the solid prosperity of many nineteenth-century farmers in the region with their well-stocked, productive farms, comfortable houses and lavish meals, were all part of the same society as the poorly-paid, ill-housed and inadequately fed labourers. It was this contrast between the splendour of the landscape, the excellence of the farms and the prosperity of the better-off classes of society on the one hand, and the wretched conditions of the working people on the other that so forcibly struck William Cobbett on his *Rural Rides* through Wiltshire in 1826. For example, Cobbett rode down the valley of the Avon from Amesbury to Salisbury and wrote with enthusiasm of the high standards of the farming that he saw, of the quality of the livestock, the well-filled rickyards and comfortable farms, and of his shame 'at beholding the general *extreme poverty* of those who cause this vale to produce such quantities of food and raiment.' He was similarly delighted by the countryside and the farming between Salisbury and Warminster and wrote that

It is impossible for the eyes of man to be fixed on a finer country than that between the village of Codford and town of Warminster; and it is not very easy for the eyes of man to discover labouring people more miserable.

One of the earliest comprehensive enquiries into the conditions of daily life for the poorer classes of society was made by Sir Frederic Morton Eden at the end of the eighteenth century and published under the title *The State of the Poor* in 1797. Eden provides a wealth of detailed information about the domestic conditions and daily life of labourers in both the towns and villages of the region during the period of upheaval caused by the Napoleonic Wars. In Somerset, for example, he described the conditions of the clothworkers at Frome, where the war had increased the demand for cloth, and noted that

The town is very ancient, and has been the seat of woollen manufacture for several centuries; yet the external appearance of the town does not indicate that wealth which is usually attendant on commerce. The houses are very different from the elegant dwellings that are to be found in the Yorkshire manufacturing towns or their neighbourhood. The streets are narrow, unpaved and dirty. There are 36 ale-houses, which it is estimated dispose of 6,700 hogsheads of strong beer annually.

A good indication of the ordinary diet of labourers and their families can be obtained from the details which Eden recorded of the food consumed both by typical families and in the parish poor-house, an institution which, unlike the union workhouses founded after 1834, did not set out to provide a diet which was deliberately of a lower standard than that generally available to the poor. Bread was by far the most important single item of diet for the working class, followed by cheese, potatoes and beer, with small quantities of meat, butter, vegetables, milk, tea and sugar. At Minehead, for example, the diet in the poor-house consisted of:

BREAKFAST: Bread and beer on Sundays.
                 Broth on all other days.
DINNER: Beef or mutton on Sundays and Thursday.
                 Fried greens, potatoes and bread on Mondays, Wednesdays and Saturdays.
                 Oatmeal, boiled water and meat on Tuesdays and Fridays.
SUPPER: Bread and beer or bread and cheese.

At Seend and many other parishes in Wiltshire Eden found that the families of labourers had been badly hit by the introduction of spinning-machines which had deprived them of an important by-employment for the women and children and of a valuable subsidiary income,

. . . since the introduction of machinery hand spinning has fallen into disuse. The Clothier no longer depends on the Poor for the yarn formerly spun at home, since he finds that 50 persons . . . with machinery can do as much as 500 without them, and the Poor from the great reduction in price scarcely have the heart to earn the little that can be made . . . so that their maintenance must chiefly depend on the exertions of the men, whose wages have not increased in proportion.

At Petersfield in Hampshire Eden found that the labourers' wages were seven shillings a week in 1794 and had increased to nine shillings in 1796. He found the parish poor-house particularly well run and closely supervised by the overseer, '. . . to his good management the reduction of the rates is principally ascribable.' Again the diet in the poor-house was no doubt similar to, if not better than, the ordinary diet of labourers outside, and consisted of the following:

BREAKFAST: Bread and milk
DINNER: Pickled pork, pudding and vegetables on Sundays, Wednesdays and Fridays.
                 Cold meat etc. on Mondays.
                 Bread and cheese on Tuesdays, Thursdays and Saturdays.
SUPPER: Bread and cheese.

'Half a pound of cheese a week is allowed to each grown person. Bread is not weighed. Sometimes, instead of pork or bacon, a little coarse beef is bought for the Poor.

In Dorset, Eden commented upon the effects of 'engrossing' or amalgamation of farms and the effects of this upon the small-holders who were evicted from their farms. At Blandford Forum he wrote 'The rapid rise of the Poor's Rates in this parish is generally attributed to the high price of provisions, the smallness of wages, and the consolidation of small farms, and the consequent depopulation of villages, which obliges small farmers to turn labourers or servants. . . .' Eden also described the domestic economy of a labourer's family at Blandford. The family consisted of a labourer aged 52, one daughter aged 18 who kept house for him, another daughter of 8, and two sons aged 6 and 3; his wife had died shortly before Eden's visit. The man earned six shillings a week in winter, seven shillings a week in summer and slightly more during harvest. The children earned nothing, and the family were dependent upon the parish to pay their house-rent and for occasional sums in poor relief. For clothing they relied upon gifts from neighbours. Their food consisted of:

BREAKFAST: Tea or Bread and cheese. DINNER AND SUPPER: Bread and Cheese, or potatoes, sometimes mashed with fat from broth, and sometimes with salt alone.

Bullock's cheek is generally bought every week to make broth. Treacle is used to sweeten tea instead of sugar. Very little milk or beer is used.

This family was chosen by Eden as typical of the rural labouring poor, and was not selected as being especially badly off. Similar evidence of the poverty and poor conditions of rural labourers can be seen from the inventories of the goods and chattels which occasionally survive. For example, the goods which a farm labourer, John Parfery, possessed in his two-roomed cottage at Chew Magna in Somerset were listed in February 1796. In his bedroom he had the bed with its bedding and a square wooden box. In the kitchen there was a square table, three chairs and a bench, one pail, one iron frying-pan, six pewter plates, three earthenware pans, one brass candlestick, one iron pot with the pot-hangings, a tin kettle, a tea-pot with three dishes and four saucers, one spade, one hand-saw and a sweeping brush. This together with his clothing made up his entire possessions.

But at the same time, during the Napoleonic Wars, there were many sections of rural society which were doing well out of the war and out of the high prices for corn and other products. The wealth and prosperity of many of the larger farmers in the region at this time can still be seen reflected in the many fine houses and farm buildings which date from the early years of the nineteenth century, and this period also witnessed great progress in agricultural improvements, in enclosures, increased yields, improved stock and the bringing of new land under cultivation. Landlords also benefited from the increase in farm-rents which such improvements made possible, and from the higher rents which resulted from the extinguishing of the old copyhold tenures and the granting of new leases at much increased rents on the enlarged farms, created after the enclosure of common fields and often also after the amalgamation of several small-holdings. This process of amalgamation of farms continued in the region after the end of the Napoleonic Wars, and had very important social consequences, with the disappearance of the small farms, or those who possessed only grazing rights, the depopulation of villages and the increase in the number of people dependent wholly or in part upon poor relief. In Wiltshire for example, an examination of 40 parishes during the period 1781 to 1831 shows that there was a decline of one eighth in the number of farmers, a decline far more marked in the corn-growing chalkland area than it was in the clay lands, where the smaller farms continued to provide economic units. A similar process was apparent in Dorset and was commented upon by the poet William Barnes, who was a perceptive observer of the rural scene:

> Then ten good deäries [dairies] were a-ved
> Along that water's windén bed,
> An' in the lewth o' hills and' wood
> A half a score farm-housen stood:
> But now,—count all o'm how you would,
> So many less do hold the land,—
> You'd vind but vive that still do stand,
> A-comèn down vrom gramfer's.

The depression which followed the Napoleonic Wars, particularly in corn prices, hit the farm labourers and their families in many parts of the south and west of England very hard indeed. Wages failed to keep pace with rising prices, and conditions were desperate for many families. For example, the labourers on the Wiltshire chalklands had especially low wages, but during the war under the impetus of the high corn prices these had risen from six or seven shillings per week in 1794 to eight shillings by 1804, and to twelve shillings a week by 1814. But by 1817 wages were back to seven or eight shillings and remained at this level during the next 25 years.

In 1843 Parliament appointed a commission to enquire into the employment of women and children in agriculture, and the evidence presented to the commissioners provides much detail about rural conditions at that time. For example one witness was Rachel Hayward, the wife of John Hayward, a farm labourer of Stourpaine in Dorset. She gave evidence about the appallingly crowded conditions in which the family lived, as well as about their meagre diet:

There are eleven of us in our family—myself, my husband, three daughters and six sons. We have two rooms, one down stairs and the other up stairs over it. We all sleep in the bedroom. My husband gets 8s or 7s a week; my two eldest daughters get about 3s 6d a week at buttoning, and three of my boys get 5s a week together; in all about 16s 6d a week. We have 16½ lugs of potato-ground on which we grow potatoes and few vegetables; for that we pay 7s 7d a year rent. We pay 1s a week for the cottage, and coal and wood cost us 1s 8d a week at this time of year (December). We get ¾ cwt of coal a week. I buy besides, every week ¾ lb soap, 1 oz tea, ½ lb bacon. I reckon we eat a pound of bread each day; that with potatoes gives us enough. My three boys that are out at work went out at nine years old.

This family was evidently greatly helped by the daughters' by-employment of button-making which was very common in that part of Dorset, and by their potato ground. Some farmers allowed their labourers to have small plots of ground to grow potatoes without charging them any rent. This was very useful to the families, but was not always total benevolence on the part of the farmers, since it meant that during the summer and autumn, while alternative employment was available elsewhere, the labourer and his family were unlikely to leave the farm, since they would then lose their potato crop.

The combination of low wages, insufficient winter employment, lack of alternatives to agriculture, limited mobility and large families meant that conditions for farm labourers in the region remained bleak throughout the nineteenth century. Sir James Caird's enquiry into English agriculture in 1850–51 provides further evidence of the low standards of housing and diet of the labourers. Caird's description of the diet of a typical labourer on Salisbury Plain is worth quoting at some length:

After doing up his horses he takes breakfast, which is made of flour with a little butter, and water 'from the tea-kettle' poured over it. He takes with him to the field a piece of bread and (if he has not a young family, and can afford it) cheese to eat at mid-day. He returns home in the afternoon to a few potatoes, and possibly a little bacon, though only those who are better off can afford this. The supper very commonly consists of bread and water. The appearance of the labourers showed, as might be expected from such a meagre diet, a want of that vigour and activity which mark the well-fed ploughman of the northern and midland counties. Beer is given by the master in hay-time and harvest. Some farmers allow ground for planting potatoes to their labourers, and carry home their fuel—which on the downs, where there is no wood, is a very expensive article in a labourer's family. . . . We found a prevalent desire for emigration among the labourers . . . .

Richard Jefferies, who wrote with such intimate knowledge of Wiltshire farming and farm labourers during the nineteenth century in his classic work *Hodge and his Masters,* also attributed the slowness and lack of vigour of the labourers to their poor diet. In a letter to *The Times* in 1872 Jefferies wrote of the Wiltshire labourer that his diet was mainly bread and cheese and that 'His food may, perhaps, have something to do with the deadened slowness which seems to pervade everything he does—there seems a lack of vitality about him.'

HOUSING

In 1867 another Parliamentary commission was appointed, this time to enquire into the 'Employment of Children and Young Persons and Women in Agriculture'. This also produced a mass of evidence about the domestic and daily life of working people. For example, on housing conditions, one of the commissioners, the Hon. E. Stanhope, reported of Dorset that

. . . the cottages of this county are more ruinous and contain worse accommodation than those in any other county I have visited, except Shropshire; . . . The estate of Lord Rivers, . . . is notorious for its bad cottages. And such villages as Bere Regis, Fordington, Winfrith, Cranbourne, or Charminster (in which there is an average of 7 persons to a house) . . . are a disgrace to the owners of the land, and contain many cottages unfit for human habitation.

Stanhope also commented upon the neglect in the villages of the most elementary sanitary precautions. 'In village after village the answer was "there is nothing like one privy to every cottage." I saw whole rows of cottages with none, and abounding with nuisances of all kinds. Remonstrance is generally disregarded, and the state of filth, in which many parishes are left, calls aloud for some active interference to relieve the present authorities of a responsibility they have grossly neglected.'

The effect of this absence of even the most rudimentary sanitary arrangements for many labourers' cottages, coupled with the over-crowded conditions, lack of adequate ventilation and the dampness of many of the dwellings, inevitably led to rheumatism, tuberculosis, bronchitis and many other diseases. Some of these rural cottages must have presented a most unwholesome spectacle of dirt and squalor, and it is important to set this against some of the more idealised views of nineteenth-century country life. The mid-nineteenth-century Bristol surveyor and land-agent, William Sturge, who was as familiar with the slums of Bristol as with the villages of north Somerset, was in no doubt that conditions in the villages were often worse than those in the towns, and that because of the bad drainage, over-crowding and general filth 'A country village is in consequence often far more unhealthy than the town'.

Some of the large estates had been active in improving the housing-conditions for their workers, and the new estate cottages of the mid-nineteenth century, with their typical architectural features, high gables, elaborate decoration and 'rustic' character, and all built to the same plan, are to be seen in many villages and hamlets throughout the region. William Cobbett had, for example, been struck by the appearance of Earl's Stoke in Wiltshire in 1826

. . . I came to a hamlet called Earl's Stoke, the houses of which stand at a few yards from each other, on the two sides of the road; every house is white; and the front of every one is covered with some sort of clematis, or with rose-trees or jasmines. It was easy to guess that the whole belonged to one owner . . . .

But the Parliamentary Report of 1867, which has already been quoted, makes it clear that the labourers' houses in a great many villages remained unaffected by any 'improvement', and that conditions in many of them were appalling, even though many no doubt looked 'picturesque' enough from the exterior and to the casual observer. At Cerne Abbas, for example, the parliamentary commissioners found that the cottages were

Very poor: most of them are thatched. There is scarcely one with three bedrooms; most have two, but the separation is often very indifferent indeed. Rooms in most cases very low, hardly six feet, and the windows are very often not made to open. In these cottages the sanitary arrangements were very bad, one privy often serving five or six cottages.

At Winfrith it was observed of the cottages that 'Almost all are wretched. As a rule they have one bedroom and a small landing place at the stairhead. In some cases the flooring is so bad that the water stands in it in rainy weather. The great number have no privies'. Some improvements were noted by the commissioners, particularly in villages belonging to large estates. For example at Wimborne St Giles the Earl of Shaftesbury had rebuilt the cottages which were said to be excellent, and at Cranborne Lord Salisbury had greatly improved some of the cottages though some which were let by copyhold tenure for lives remained very bad. Generally the housing conditions for labourers throughout the chalkland region of Dorset, Wiltshire and Hampshire were found to be deplorable. The situation was somewhat better in Somerset, and throughout the claylands, where there were more small, family farms and where dairy-farming provided a very different kind of agricultural environment. Moreover in north Somerset and the Mendip area the proximity of Bristol and the existence of alternative forms of employment in coal- and lead-mining or in the cloth trade served to keep wages at a higher level. For example, the parliamentary commissioners in 1867 several times noted the influence of alternative employments: 'Wages have risen in consequence of the railway coming' (Stanton Drew); '. . . men and boys get such good wages in the mines, that it is not necessary for women to work at all out of doors' (Radstock); 'The men go up to work at the lead mines on Mendip' (Compton Martin). In these areas there were few examples of the grossly inadequate cottages found on the chalklands, although many cottages were found to be very crowded. This was a particular problem in any neighbourhood where employment was available and to which men were therefore attracted. At Clevedon, for example, where work was available in the rapidly growing resort, Sir Arthur Elton of Clevedon Court had built several new, improved cottages on his estate, but his land-agent stated that this had done little to relieve over-crowding since '. . . people who have a good cottage with three bedrooms will often take in as many as eight lodgers, and herd with their families in the kitchen.'

This chapter has deliberately concentrated attention particularly upon the domestic conditions of the poorest section of the rural community, because it is the rural labourers which are so often forgotten or ignored in conventional accounts of village communities. But in seeking to redress this balance, and in pointing out the vast discrepancy between the wealth and conditions of daily life of the gentry and land-owning class or the farmers on the one hand and that of the farm workers upon whose labours they ultimately depended on the other, it would be quite wrong to give the impression that rural society consisted only of these two, so dissimilar, elements. The great contrast between rural society at any time during the period from 1500 to 1900 and the rural communities of the twentieth century, is how very self contained and self-supporting even quite small communities were, and what a wide range of craftsmen and traders were to be found in all the villages. A glance at any nineteenth-century directory is sufficient to show this very clearly. Rural society consisted not only of those engaged in farming but comprised also that army of craftsmen, shopkeepers, carters, carriers, blacksmiths, carpenters, innkeepers, millers and others who provided the services necessary both to agriculture and to community life. Nor must we forget the vast number of household servants which a close examination of any community before the end of the nine-teenth century reveals. The standard of living of most of these people, far below that of even the minor gentry or farmers, was generally much higher than that of the farm labourers.

The social life of the communities, and the way in which they provided for the religious, educational, charitable and recreational needs of their inhabitants, will be considered in Chapter 6.

5. Markets, fairs and travel

Of vital importance in both the economic and social life of rural communities were the weekly markets and annual fairs. This chapter will be concerned with the place of these institutions in the life of the region, and also with the facilities that existed for travel and for the transport of goods, and the way in which these improved during the period. Markets and fairs originally served different functions; markets were weekly occasions for buying and selling and were to be found in towns and villages throughout the region, while fairs served much larger, seasonal needs, often existed outside towns or villages on hill-tops or open spaces, attracted custom from a much wider area, and often also had a much more strongly marked social role for the rural communities which they served. Both markets and fairs present great problems for the historian, since so much of the business transacted at them has left no written record at all, and it is therefore impossible to know of more than a very few of all the millions of business transactions which were conducted at them.

MARKETS

Before the coming of the railways and the growth of numerous permanent shops, there were a large number of weekly markets held in towns and villages throughout the region, and few places, even the most remote, were more than ten miles from a market. From contemporary directories and other sources it is possible to count the number of markets in each county at various times, as follows:

	1500–1650	1690	1702	1720	1792	1888
DORSET	21	22	20	15	17	11
HAMPSHIRE	21	25	—	—	19	6
SOMERSET	39	42	30	25	32	13
WILTSHIRE	23	23	23	20	20	9

This table shows very clearly the large number of markets in each county during the earlier part of the period 1500–1900 and the sharp decline in numbers which occurred in the nineteenth century with the development of improved roads and methods of travel and, in particular, with the coming of the railways. The result of this decline is still to be seen in many former market towns and villages throughout the region, where the market place which was once the busy hub and focus for the whole area now stands forlornly deserted or has been encroached upon by later buildings. The little market houses which once sheltered the sellers of eggs, poultry, butter, fish and a host of other wares are still to be seen in many places, sometimes now turned to other uses, and the lock-ups which once accommodated those who had over-indulged themselves at the market inns also survive in many towns and villages.

Most of the markets held in the little towns and villages were very small and possessed no more than a local significance, but a few were much larger, attracted custom from long distances, and often also specialised in particular commodities. For example, the markets in that area where Somerset, Dorset, Wiltshire and Hampshire converge—and where the corn-growing chalkland region and the dairy farming, cloth-producing claylands meet—at places such as Shaftesbury, Salisbury, Wilton, Warminster, Wincanton and Bruton, were all very important during the earlier part of the period in the process whereby grain was transferred from one region to another. John Aubrey wrote of Warminster in the mid-seventeenth century that 'It is held to be the greatest corn-market by much in the West of England'; and in the early nineteenth century Cobbett wrote that 'It is a great corn-market: one of the greatest in this part of England. . . .' During the 1630s a government enquiry found that the two markets at Bruton and Wincanton supplied corn to nearly 7,000 people in the surrounding cloth-making districts, and that most of this corn came from the Dorset and Wiltshire chalklands. Marlborough and Hindon in Wiltshire were also very important corn markets during the seventeenth and eighteenth centuries; Aubrey described Hindon as 'the second best market after Warminster in the county.' Marlborough was also an important cheese market, as was also Yeovil and Wincanton. Large weekly cattle markets attracting more than purely local custom were held at Alton, Blandford Forum, Bridgwater, Crewkerne, Devizes, Dunster, Highworth, Market Lavington, Sherborne, Swindon and Taunton. Important sheep markets were held at Alresford, Blandford, Crewkerne and Hindon, though sheep were much more commonly sold at the great seasonal sheep fairs which will be discussed later. Glastonbury and Langport, set among the

Somerset levels, were famous for wildfowl, while Bridport and Yeovil had important hemp markets and Ilminster and Shaftesbury were noted for leather. In the cloth-producing areas there were cloth markets at Frome, Shepton Mallet and Taunton. But most markets in the region had no specialities, and were entirely devoted to the needs of the little rural communities which they served. For a few markets evidence survives concerning the trade conducted at them which also gives some indication of the crowded conditions, bustle and atmosphere of the market. At Yeovil, for example, the very busy market was important for much of north-west Dorset and for south Somerset. The churchwardens' accounts for the sixteenth century show that a major source of income for the church was the payments received from traders for the use of the weights and measures which were kept in the church, and which no doubt gave confidence to purchasers at a time long before weights and measures were standardised throughout the country. During the early seventeenth century Thomas Gerard, who lived nearby at Trent and would have known the Yeovil market well, wrote that

The market, of a little towne, is one of the greatest I have seene . . . the greatest commodity is cheese, which being made in greate abundance in the adjoyninge country is weekly transported hence both into Wilts and Hampshire in a very greate quantity; hemp and linen thread are very good chafer (trade) with them too.

Much detail about the trade of the market at Yeovil and about its rapid growth during the sixteenth and early seventeenth centuries emerges from a long and involved dispute there over the profits of the market, the right to erect stalls and standings in the streets, over the regulation of the market and over the rights of the inhabitants of the neighbouring manor of Hendford. It is clear from the mass of evidence produced by both sides in the dispute that besides butter, cheese, hemp, linen and leather, large numbers of cattle, sheep and horses were sold at the market each week, as well as vegetables, hops and a variety of trinkets sold by itinerant pedlars and chapmen. The market evidently formed the major focal point for the large and fertile agricultural region surrounding it.

Disputes over rights in the market also provided a good deal of incidental information about the one at Shaftesbury, which was the busiest of the Dorset markets and one of the most frequented of all the markets in the region during the sixteenth and seventeenth centuries. On its commanding hill-top position, the town occupied an especially advantageous situation, mid-way between the rich claylands of the Blackmoor Vale and the rolling chalk downlands of Hampshire, Wiltshire and Dorset. In addition,

Shaftesbury was on the important route from London to the West of England, as well as being on the road between Bristol and Poole. It is an indication of the former importance of the town that, despite its hill-top position, Shaftesbury still has more roads radiating from it than any other town in Dorset. In 1632 it was stated that '. . . there is greater store of corn vented in that towne (Shaftesbury) from the hill country into Blackmore and some parts of Somersetshire than in any three townes in this county (Dorset) . . . for that this town standeth in the midway between the hill and the vale.' On market days and during the annual fairs there was great congestion in the streets of Shaftesbury, and throughout the sixteenth, seventeenth and eighteenth centuries there were disputes about obstruction caused by standings, and arguments between stallholders and travellers through the town. In 1620, for example, the mayor ordered that some of the stalls in the main street were to be pulled down because 'the same street is a Common way as well for Carts and Carriages as for travellers on horsebacke and on Foot from London to the Mount westwards' and the stalls 'are a great annoyance to the corn market there and to buyers and sellers of corn and victual there and a straitening unto the usual travelling way through the said market and dangerous for travellers and a hindrance to the market men there.' The stall-holders were told to 'goe to places more convenient for uttering theire wares' within the town, but many of them were unwilling to leave the main street, 'and ill language giving to the said maior by some of them.' Before long the stalls were back again, and the complaints and congestion continued as before.

Another court case over the market in the early seventeenth century produced a vast quantity of evidence concerning the size and importance of the market at Shaftesbury. One resident stated that 'there is usually brought into the market place there on market days sometimes forty carts of corn, sometimes more, sometimes less, besides divers horse loads of corn brought thither also to be sold.' Others mentioned the very large numbers of cattle, sheep and swine which were offered for sale each week, and the quantity of other agricultural products which were sold—meat, poultry, butter, cheese, fruit and vegetables. It is evident that people came to the market from all over north-east Dorset and south-west Wiltshire as well as from as far away as Trowbridge and Devizes. At the Shaftesbury market there was a market-house near St Peter's church where the town scales and weights were kept, and a corn market which was '. . . a faire building made with timber and covered with lead . . . and a bell to ring when the said market shall begin.' In addition, there was a butter cross which had been built about 1570 by the mayor, Edmund Bower, 'for all those who sold butter, cheese, eggs, poultry or the like to stand or sit dry in during the market,' as well as fish, cheese, and poultry crosses which had also been erected during the sixteenth century. Cattle and swine were sold on Gold Hill, the steep thoroughfare leading down from St Peter's church, and moveable pens were erected along the streets for the sheep sales. There were also a few permanent shops which had been erected during the sixteenth century and were known as Chapman's Standings. As well as agricultural products there is mention also of a great range of other wares being offered for sale—fish, ironware, candles, besoms, gloves, salt, leather, cloth, etc. The town also contained 24 licensed inns and alehouses, some of them very large establishments, for the accommodation and entertainment of travellers and market-men alike. For a traveller from London, hurrying on to the west, the bustle, obstructions and confusion of the Shaftesbury streets on a market day must have meant a considerable hindrance and delay: but to the farmers of a wide area it represented the major outlet for much of their produce. A similar situation would have confronted the traveller through a score of other west-country market-places on their market days—Blandford Forum, Bridgwater, Devizes, Dorchester, Marlborough, Salisbury, Somerton, Taunton, Warminster, Yeovil and many others. Each also fulfilled the same crucial role in the economic and social life of its surrounding area.

Such markets as these, with an influence throughout the local community and beyond, reached the peak of their importance during the seventeenth century, and thereafter began to decline. There were several reasons for this: the coming of better roads, and later of canals and railways, meant that many of the small, purely local markets declined rapidly, as did also those in places which were missed by the railways network. But in many places the decline of the market had begun long before this, and was brought about by other factors. Some smaller markets were engulfed by their larger neighbours, as for example the market at Glastonbury which was diminished during the early eighteenth century by the rising attraction of Somerton, or that at Frampton in Dorset which was overwhelmed by the superior attractions of nearby Dorchester. Other small markets suffered from plague or fire, as for example Steeple Ashton, where a fire caused the removal of the market to Market Lavington; or Bere Regis and Beaminster where fires severely curtailed the markets. The markets at Blandford Forum and Bridport were badly affected by outbreaks of plague during the later seventeenth century, and plague caused the removal of the important cattle market at Highworth to a new site at Swindon. When during the reign of Elizabeth the city of Bath was 'infected and greatly visited with the plague, in such sort as the inhabitants of the country bordering upon . . . Bath did stay their repair to the said city upon the market days . . .', the market for wool, yarn and other merchandise was for a time moved to Marshfield over the border in Gloucestershire. Another major reason for the decline of some markets was that the tolls which were charged led many traders to forsake the open markets and instead to make private deals upon which tolls could not be levied. This practice was, naturally, vigorously resisted by the authorities in the market towns who depended upon the tolls for a large part of the town's revenue, and by those private owners of markets, lords of manors and others for whom tolls in their markets were a major source of income. At Devizes in 1699 the Common Council received complaints that 'divers quantities and parcels of flesh, cheese, wool and woollen yarne . . . have not of late been carried to and weighed att the several and respective Common Beames . . . to the prejudice and loss of the said Maior and Burgesses of the said Borough and theire Tennants of the said faires and marketts.' Similarly at Dorchester in 1693 it was stated that large quantities of corn were being sold privately in inns and alehouses, thus avoiding both the tolls and the supervision of the justices to which the transactions would have been subject in the open market. Many other similar instances are to be found of this retreat from the regulations and exactions of the open market which was a major cause of decline in many markets long before the coming of the railways. William Cobbett noted approvingly at Warminster in 1826 that

. . . here things are still conducted in the good old honest fashion. The corn is brought and pitched in the market before it is sold; and when it is sold, it is paid for on the nail . . . . Almost everywhere else the corn is sold by sample; it is sold by juggling in a corner; . . . there is no fair and open market . . .

Dealings in livestock were also increasingly carried on outside markets in private bargains and through dealers and, as will be shown later, sheep in particular were often driven very long distances to be sold. An example of the way in which dealers could monopolise markets over a wide area is shown in a complaint made to the Wiltshire justices in 1634 about the activities of various sheep dealers in Wiltshire who, it was alleged,

. . . continually goe from Faire to Faire, and from Markett to Markett, from Sheepefould to Sheepefould, from one man to another, where they buie continually great numbers of Sheepe: as for example one Saterday to the market at Blandford Forum, the Wensday following sell the same againe at Wilton. Nay, they and the most of them will buie one day and sell the same againe the next, nay, buie and sell in one and the same day, insomuch that our Fayres and Markets are for the most part furnished by these sort of jobbers and Ingrossers . . . .

It was complained that these dealers had totally monopolised some markets and that they 'have not been ashamed to brage and boast that they have sould this yeare last past 6,000, 5,000, 4,000 and 3,000 sheepe, some more some lesse. . . .' The result of the decline and eventual extinction of so many of the markets in the area can still be seen by the most casual observer in the number of little market-towns which now lack their markets, and in the number of former market-places to be seen in so many of the towns and villages of the region.

FAIRS

Turning from the regular weekly markets to the annual, seasonal fairs, many of these were found not in towns or villages but on some quite isolated open site, as, for example, at Whitedown Hill in south Somerset, Woodbury Hill near Bere Regis, Tan Hill and Yarnbury Castle in Wiltshire, or Weyhill near Andover, though others were held in towns and villages and sometimes at places which did not have weekly markets. Like the markets, many of the fairs were of no more than local significance, but a few attracted custom from very long distances. Moreover the markets and fairs were not important simply as centres of trade; they also provided an occasion for meetings, exchange of news, of ideas on politics, farming improvements and other topics, as well as an opportunity for social diversion. An indication of the distance to which the influence of a fair could extend is shown in the partial record which survives of dealings at Whitedown Fair, which was held each year during Whit-week on Whitedown Hill between Chard and Crewkerne, a few miles over the Dorset border in Somerset. People came to this fair from all over west Dorset and from a large area of Somerset, and a few traders came from much further afield, including some dealers from Wales who regularly came to sell cattle there. The influence of Woodbury Hill Fair in Dorset is shown in the way in which the date of the Fair was used in manorial and other documents as a cardinal point of the year, and 'Woodbury Day' was used instead of a date in the common field and grazing regulations of manors at a considerable distance from the site of the Fair. For example, the phrase is commonly used in the manorial records of Piddletrenthide which is more than ten miles away, and of Wyke Regis which is more than 15 miles distant, as well as in the records of many nearer manors. The phrase also occurs frequently in the Quarter Sessions records, and the date of the Fair was evidently of great importance in Dorchester, for in September 1648 a public thanks-giving in the town was postponed because 'it falls out to be on Woodbury Fair Eve, at which time most of the Towne will be from home.'

Unfortunately, in spite of the importance of markets and fairs, com-paratively few records have survived, either concerning the business transacted or on their role in the social life of the communities they served. One source which does give some indication of the crowds, the atmosphere and the conditions of Woodbury Hill Fair, and of its attraction for people from all over Dorset and for traders from all over south and west England, is a notebook kept by Francis Ashley, the recorder of Dorchester and one of the county justices of the peace, concerning the people who were tried or examined before him during the years from 1614 to 1635. Each year in September, Ashley recorded a fresh crop of thieves, cut-purses and tricksters of all kinds who were brought before him after having been arrested at the fair. Ashley's notes give interesting information about the people who came to the fair, and about the underworld of petty criminals who frequented such occasions. Many of those brought before Ashley, both accused and witnesses, had travelled very long distances to attend the fair. For example, Margaret Hill, an arras-weaver of Aldergate in London was brought before him in September 1617, accused of stealing purses at the fair, and testimony was given by William Kent of Salisbury, 'hard-wareman', and Michael Farringdon of Coventry 'linen-draper', both of whom had standings at the fair. At the same time, several other persons were tried for stealing goods, being drunk and disorderly or for unlawful gaming and fortune-telling at the fair. In 1620 Robert Watkins, a cook and baker from London who had set up a stall selling refreshments at the fair, was accused of 'having made such a fire at 12 o'clock at night that he (the night watchman) was in feare that he would set the booths afire'. Watkins was also accused of fortune-telling and illegal gaming. Evidence in this case was given by Robert How, a chapman or pedlar of St Albans, who stated that he had come to Woodbury Hill by way of markets and fairs at Newbury, Winchester and Salisbury. Mention was also made of the tem-porary booths, shelters, standings and tents which were erected on the hill-top, as well as of 'a bower for people to lodge in for the night, lying upon hides of tanned leather that were in the Bower.' Other cases upon which Ashley made notes contained references to tents erected on the hill where meals and ale could be purchased, to the sheep and cattle pens, and to the sale of horses, butter, cheese, cloth, canvas, haberdashery, lace and leather goods, as well as the various trinkets sold by the petty chapmen. Other traders mentioned included a mercer from Honiton in Devon, two chapmen from Coventry, a weaver from Devon who had come to the fair to sell cloth and to buy cheese, a shoemaker and a pack-saddle maker from Wells, bonelace sellers from Berkshire and Oxfordshire, as well as people from all over Dorset and the neighbouring counties. The case is also recorded by Ashley of a yeoman farmer from Lidlinch who went to Stalbridge fair in August 1634 to sell some cattle. Having made his sale, he bought himself a dinner in a booth at the fair, and then, no doubt pleased with his deal and with money in his pocket, he bought some pears to take home to his children. It was while doing this that he caught a thief in the act of picking his pocket. The thief proved to be Thomas Perkins, a groom from Chesilton in Berkshire, and evidence in the case was given by a petty chapman from Thame in Oxfordshire as well as by several Dorset farmers.

Ashley also records an example of the sort of trickery which the rogues who travelled from fair to fair could perpetrate on unsuspecting people. David Morgan of Stony Stratford in Berkshire, who described himself as a cutler, had come to Woodbury Hill in September 1634 via London, and fairs at Bristol, Salisbury, Southampton and Farnham. He had brought some knives to Woodbury Hill to sell, but evidently depended for his livelihood mainly on trickery, unlawful gaming and petty crimes. Evidence was given concerning one incident when Morgan was said to have encountered a group of people who were eating tripe

and begged of them some of their Tripes, which they willingly gave him; then he, to requite their kindness, told them that he would sell them a good bargaine, and showed them forth a piece of Cambricke, telling them that they should have itt for five shillings, itt being of greter valew; which bargaine the said company well liking of delivered him 5s for the same, but he stepped aside and folded up the Tripe which they had given him in cleane paper in the same manner that the Cambricke was before folded, and delivered itt to the said company in steed of the Cambricke; And soe made them pay five shillings for their owne Tripe.

An important fair for wool and yarn was held in Somerset each year at Norton St Philip. Like many other west-country fairs this one coincided with the patronal festival of the parish church, and each year for several days on either side of the feast of S.S. Philip and James (1 May) the 'great house or inn called the George', was emptied of much of its furniture and was filled with the packs and bales of merchants and its 'great store of rooms' for 'lodging and entertainment' were filled with traders and customers. The greatest of all the many sheep fairs in the area was held on the downland at Weyhill near Andover in Hampshire at the junction of several ancient roads and trackways. In 1683 more than 30,000 sheep were said to have been sold at Weyhill, and early in the eighteenth century Defoe, who described it as 'the greatest fair for sheep . . . that this nation can shew', despaired of estimating the number of sheep he saw being sold there.

Inns like the George at Norton St Philip played a very important part in the marketing process, providing meeting places, exchanges, banking and storage facilities as well as food, drink and entertainment. As already mentioned, there were 24 licensed inns and alehouses at Shaftesbury in the seventeenth century, and inns were similarly important, for example, at Taunton, Devizes and Salisbury. At Salisbury in 1686 there were sufficient inns to provide accommodation for 548 travellers and 865 horses; while Taunton could accommodate 247 travellers, Wells 402, Bath 324 and Bridgwater 142.

TRAVEL

The major factor influencing the development of marketing in the region throughout the period 1500–1900 was the changes which took place in communications and methods of travel, and this subject will be considered in the final section of this chapter. Although travel was difficult and often dangerous before the improvement of the roads by turnpiking during the eighteenth century, nonetheless regular pack-horse and carrier services between most of the towns of the south-west and centres like London and Bristol were well established by the early seventeenth century, and sheep and cattle were regularly driven very long distances by drovers. The colourful descriptions of the bad state of the roads left by many travellers during the sixteenth and seventeenth centuries does not mean that the roads were not used nor that the rural communities were so isolated as is sometimes supposed. The wayfaring merchants and pedlars who attended the fairs of the region have already been noticed, and some agricultural produce was also marketed far outside the region. For example, in 1573 the Lord Mayor of London wrote of the trade in corn both by land and sea from the counties to the west of London including Wiltshire, Dorset and Hampshire,

The Cytie hathe bene chieflie furnished with all kinde of grayne for provision of the same from those shires lyenge westward from the Cytie and aptlie conveyed to the Cytie as well by lande as by the River of Thames.

Regular carrier services also operated from most of the larger towns. For example in the early seventeenth century the Earl of Suffolk's rents from his estates at Lulworth and the surrounding area in Dorset were normally sent up to London by the carriers who regularly operated from Blandford, and the carriers' waggon brought back from London fruit-trees, gunpowder, furniture and other materials as well as luxury goods for use at Lulworth. From Somerset there were several regular carrier-services to London in the seventeenth century; for example, the account book of Lord Poulett of Hinton St George near Crewkerne, which covers the years 1651–55 contains constant references to goods being sent to and from London. Regular carriers from Yeovil, Crewkerne and Chard are mentioned, as well as 'Loringe the carrier who lives at Hinton.' Loringe evidently made journeys to London every week and letters for Hinton St George could be left for him to collect in London at the Queen's Arms, Holborn Bridge. London carriers also made regular journeys to the west country, and one of these, George Clarke, who was described as 'a waggoner of Hounslow', died while he was at Hinton St George and was buried there in January 1636. Fish was also regularly carried overland by pack-horses from the Dorset coastal towns and villages to London, Devizes, Oxford and elsewhere, and during the summer months there was a regular service by boat transporting fish, oysters and lobsters from Dorset to London. A witness to the efficiency of the early seventeenth-century system of overland transport by pack-horse is provided by Walter Yonge, a Justice of the Peace and member of Parliament for Honiton, who lived at Axminster, and whose diary covering the years 1604–28 gives a graphic description of strings of pack-horses, tied head to tail, being loaded by fish jobbers with fresh fish on the beach at Lyme Regis, and of their hurried departure on the 150-mile journey to London. On their return from London the carriers and pack-horses were occasionally used to bring luxury goods— silk, haberdashery, books and imported food-stuffs—to the west country. Later in the seventeenth century John Aubrey described how fish from Poole was brought to the markets at Salisbury and Devizes, and sent on to Oxford and elsewhere. Most of the Wiltshire cloth-production from the sixteenth century onwards was also sent by road to London to be sold at Blackwell Hall.

A principal export from the west-country was the cattle and sheep which were driven live to markets in London, the home counties and elsewhere. Early in the eighteenth century Defoe commented upon the trade in live cattle between the low-lying area around Bridgwater in Somerset and London 'As the country is all a grazing, rich, feeding soil, so a great number of large oxen are fed here, which are sent up to London. . . .' Nearly a century earlier, two brothers, John and Thomas

Bull of Long Sutton in Somerset, made their livelihood during the period 1627-37 from driving cattle to the London market. Great numbers of Welsh and Irish cattle were also brought into Somerset and other parts of the region for fattening before being driven to the London market. The Wiltshire Quarter Sessions rolls record the case of Edward Gille of New Sarum, who is described as a tailor, but who had gone to Ireland in August 1639 and had spent £180 in buying cattle for shipping to England for fattening. All his cattle were, however, lost during a tempest in the Irish Channel, and Gille was reduced to penury and obliged to appeal to the Quarter Sessions for charity. In a dispute over stolen cattle which came before the Court of Star Chamber in 1623, William Brounker, a yeoman of Whaddon near Melksham in Wiltshire, stated that he was a grazier and that he frequently used 'to repayre to certen Fayres in Shropshire and the county of Radnor to buy Rother beasts (cattle) there to stocke his grounds as the Grasiers dwelling near your subject in the said county of Wilts. use to doe.' This dispute incidentally illustrates the speed at which cattle could be driven across country, for Brounker bought 50 cattle at Kington in Radnorshire on 6 May 1623 and five days later they were already on his farm in Wiltshire. The accounts of the stock kept by Lord Shaftesbury at Wimborne St Giles during the seventeenth century also show that he commonly purchased large numbers of Welsh cattle for fattening on his land.

Great numbers of west-country sheep were also driven to London and the home counties for sale, or were sold to dealers at one of the local sheep fairs and subsequently driven to the London market. During the seventeenth and eighteenth centuries a very large trade grew up with the Dorset horn breed which, because of its readiness to produce lambs very early, in time for the Christmas market, became very popular with dealers. Defoe, for example, commented on the great trade which was carried on with Dorset Horn ewes and lambs, and on the fact that they were sold in great numbers to farmers from Kent, Surrey, Buckinghamshire and Bedfordshire to be fattened for the Christmas market.

The drovers and the drove-roads along which they moved the cattle and sheep were very important in the economic life of the whole region until the coming of the railways, but curiously little documentary evidence survives about the drovers themselves. Few of them left accounts, and they were such a normal part of the agricultural scene that apart from occasional disputes and court cases, their activities have left little record although the drove-roads which they used survive as green ways, tracks and bridle-paths all over the west-country. Thousands of cattle, for example, were brought into the ports of Somerset each year from Wales and Ireland, to be fattened on the rich pastures of the Somerset levels or on the clay-lands of Wiltshire and Dorset, before being driven on to markets in Bristol, the clothing towns of Wiltshire and Somerset or farther afield as far as London. But little documentary evidence survives concerning this important trade nor on those often colourful characters, the drovers, who made their living in transporting cattle and sheep on the hoof for sale in distant markets.

From the eighteenth century onwards rural life in the region was greatly affected by three successive improvements in the transport system: turnpike roads, canals, and railways. This is not the place to re-tell the complex story of the introduction and development of each of these three systems in the Wessex region, but attention will be given instead to the effect of these improved communications upon rural life. The first improvement, the turnpike roads, had a comparatively small influence on rural life, except upon those communities through which the roads passed, and apart from the opportunities for employment which the construction and maintenance of the new and improved roads offered. The roads were designed to speed the coaches of the wealthy onward, and most members of the rural communities through which they passed were still dependent upon their own legs or upon the carrier's cart to get them to market. The new roads and the improvement of the existing roads did make the transportation of both goods and livestock easier; but rural life was much more markedly affected in those parts of the region where canals were constructed, or where river navigation was improved as along the Avon between Bristol and Bath or in Somerset along the Parrett. The effect of the canals must not be over-emphasised for they were very localised in their impact, and many parts of the region had no waterways at all. But places within easy reach of the canals were supplied with coal, stone for roads and buildings, bricks, slate, timber, salt and manure all at a much cheaper rate and in far greater abundance than would otherwise have been possible. Not all of this was pure gain, for the canals began the process, later completed by the railways, of breaking down the old regional traditions of vernacular building using local materials which generally fitted snugly into the landscape, and instead made universally available the far less attractive but cheap brick, slate and clay tiles. The canals also for the first time made it easily possible to send large quantities of corn, cheese, butter and other farm produce out of the rural areas, and greatly extended the available markets. They therefore had the same sort of effect on the agriculture of the few areas affected as the railways were later to have over a much wider area. This was particularly the case with the Kennet and Avon canal which was completed in 1810. A pamphlet issued in 1788 urging the scheme for 'extending the navigation of the rivers Kennett and Avon' had argued that by the building of the canal

The price of carriage of coals and all other articles will be greatly reduced; the estates of gentlemen and farmers will be improved at much easier expense by the introduction of free-stone, timber, brick, tile and other building materials; lime, peat-ashes, and manure of all sorts. They will find new markets for the produce of their farms and estates: corn, malt, cheese, and other productions, will meet with a ready and cheap conveyance to the great marts.

All of this proved to be true, for the canal enabled Wiltshire farmers easily and cheaply to supply Bristol and Bath in one direction and Reading and London in the other. Cobbett in 1826 commented sourly on the sight of the canal at Devizes, 'the great channel through which the produce of the country is carried away to be devoured by idlers, the thieves and the prostitutes, who are all tax-eaters in the Wens of Bath and London.' The canals also began the process, also later completed by the railways, of making easily available to farmers the new, mass-produced tools and implements, as well as drainage-pipes and other prerequisites for any further advances in agricultural techniques. The other major impact of the canals upon rural life was in the new opportunities for employment they created both in their construction and use, and in the new contacts with a wider world which they made so much more easily possible.

The railways had a much more dramatic effect upon a much wider area, for at their height there were few parts of the region which were more than a few miles from a railway. Even before they opened, the very large gangs of navvies required for the massive engineering work involved in their construction had a disruptive effect upon many of the hitherto remote rural communities through which the line passed. Moreover the railway created a large number of permanent, secure and comparatively well-paid jobs, so that it affected wage-rates in other occupations including farming. Upon agriculture itself the railways had a profound effect in bringing new equipment, new breeds of cattle, artificial fertilisers, drainage pipes, etc., and in making possible the cheap, rapid transport of farm produce. The most far-reaching effect was in creating a vastly increased market for liquid milk to supply the towns; in north Wiltshire, for example, after the coming of the railways many farmers abandoned the production of butter and cheese in favour of the liquid-milk trade. The first wholesale depot in Wiltshire devoted to supplying the London market was opened at Semley in 1871, while the Anglo-Swiss Condensed Milk Company (later Nestlé Company) opened at Chippenham in 1873. The situation was the same in the claylands of Somerset and Dorset where the railways soon became the essential lifeline of the dairy farmers, and revolutionised their existence. Less happily for the fortunes of English agriculture, the railways also made possible the easy distribution of a flood of cheap, imported foodstuffs, especially of wheat from the American and Canadian prairies, which began in earnest during the 1870s and, coinciding as it did with a run of bad harvests in England, left English arable farming prostrate. Other imports included refrigerated meat and Danish bacon and eggs. The effects of this influx of cheap foodstuffs were to be seen throughout the Wessex region in the later nineteenth century in mounting arrears of rent, bankrupt tenants, unlet farms, arable lands allowed to revert to grass or to weed and waste. In this situation, partly brought about by the effect of the railways, the sales of liquid milk and dairy products (also dependent upon the railways) provided the only bright spot. The difference in profitability between arable and dairy farming during the last quarter of the nineteenth century can be seen from the rent income on the Marquess of Bath's Longleat estate. On that part of the estate which lay in the Wiltshire chalkland, corn-growing region (about one third of the whole), rents declined by about a quarter, tenants were bankrupt and unable to pay, and many of the farms fell into hand; on the rest of the estate which lay in the clayland, dairy-farming parts of Wiltshire and around Cheddar and Frome in Somerset, there were few signs of difficulty and rents fell only a little if at all during the period. It was not of course easy, or cheap, to change quickly from arable to dairy farming, and on the Marquess of Ailesbury's Savernake estate, when large-scale dairy farming was introduced on five farms in the vale of Pewsey covering 3,500 acres during the 1890s, the average rent had to be reduced to 8s 2d per acre as against a former rent for the land as arable before the depression of 19s per acre. But for those farmers who could specialise and concentrate on liquid-milk production, it was the railways which enabled them to weather the storm.

The railways also had a dramatic effect upon the markets both in those towns and villages through which they passed, and upon those which they missed. In Dorset, for example, the coming of the railway helped to change Sherborne, Gillingham, Bridport and above all Dorchester into bustling centres of population and enterprise; while Cerne Abbas and Beaminster, avoided by the railway, declined very rapidly; their markets died and they virtually ceased to be towns at all. A similar pattern is to be observed all over the region. Finally, the railways gave a new and hitherto quite unknown mobility to rural society. The old, tightly-knit rural communities were, inevitably, shattered by the impact: the marriage registers show how the railways, and no doubt also the bicycle, led to marriages between partners who lived much farther away from each other than would have been the case a few years previously. The railways also played a crucial role in enabling many people to leave the country villages during the latter half of the nineteenth century, either to emigrate or to seek work in the towns; they were therefore a potent factor in the process of rural depopulation.

6. Social and religious life

For most of the period under review the social as well as the religious life of the rural communities of the region was centred upon the parish church. Later and for some sections of the rural population, it was focused upon one of the numerous non-conformist chapels. The central position of the parish church in both religious and social life during the sixteenth and seventeenth centuries can be seen from the surviving churchwardens' accounts and from records of the ecclesiastical courts which, for long after the Reformation, continued to exercise control over such matters as morality, church attendance and business relating to marriage and to wills. During the sixteenth century, life in all the rural communities of the region was, inevitably, greatly affected by the series of upheavals and changes which together comprised the Reformation. These changes touched many aspects of rural life, economic and social as well as religious. The dissolution of the monasteries created a massive dislocation of life in many places, for the whole region was notable for the number, size, wealth and magnificence of its monasteries, and their suppression involved not only the ruin of the buildings and churches, but the destruction also of many of the opportunities for employment, education and charity which they had provided; above all, the dissolution brought a wholesale change in land ownership. For many little communities which had been wholly or partly dependent upon a large monastic institution in their midst the results of the dissolution were disastrous, as for example Cerne Abbas, Abbotsbury, Keynsham, Bruton, Lacock, Wilton and many other similar places. It says much for the way in which the monastic institutions had lost public sympathy and support that in a region so thickly spread with monasteries, large and small, there was not a single protest movement against the dissolution.

PARISH CHURCHES

In the parish churches the religious changes of the sixteenth century involved great alterations in the furnishing and interior appearance of the buildings, as well as in the services and the theology. These changes ordered by each successive edict of the government at Westminster, and duly carried out by the churchwardens in each parish, can be seen reflected in many churchwardens' accounts for the period. For example, at Yatton in North Somerset the accounts which survive from the fifteenth century show how the people of that community had lavished care, love and money upon the fabric, furnishing and decoration of their magnificent parish church. The records show in particular the way in which the construction of a huge, elaborately-carved and decorated rood screen dividing the nave from the chancel had been arranged and paid for by the parishioners during the fifteenth century with money raised from gifts, bequests, parish collections and 'church-ales' or parochial festivities. During the sixteenth century the Yatton accounts, like those of many other parishes in the region, reveal how during the early years of the century the church was a blaze of colour and lights, with many statues, finely carved benches and screens, wall-paintings, books, manuscripts, vestments, curtains, hangings for the altar and many other precious things. During the course of the sixteenth century, most of these things were removed, defaced or destroyed. The Yatton accounts show how the churchwardens responded immediately and apparently without question to every twist and change of government policy throughout the century. In 1538, for example, in response to the government's instructions, the churchwardens purchased a large volume of the bible in English and began to keep registers of all baptisms, marriages and burials conducted in the church. Further minor changes in furnishings and decorations occurred during the early 1540s, and then in 1548 the churchwardens paid 5d for 'taking down the images in the church'—in other words for removing all the statues, most of which had been bought by the parishioners during the previous century. In the same year, the stone altars were dug out and replaced by wooden tables and in 1549 the first book of common prayer was purchased, while the Latin mass was replaced by the service in English. In 1549 also, the churchwardens, realising the wholesale confiscation from parish churches of things of value which royal policy was about to order, took the remarkable step of selling the valuable silver cross which had stood on the high altar and spending the money upon making a defence against floods which were always a danger in that low-lying coastal area. The accounts record simply that

This yere the sylver crosse of our church was sold and the money of the sayd crosse was bestowyd upon the makying of a sirten stlusse or yere (a certain sluice or weir) agenste the rage of ye salt water.

This is an unusual example of foresight upon the part of parish church-wardens, most of whom meekly delivered up the valuables of the churches to the King's commissioners. The Yatton accounts also show how in 1553 when Queen Mary came to the throne the churchwardens, apparently without question, restored the Latin mass, rebuilt the old stone altars and purchased afresh many of the items which had been swept away a few years previously, such as the Latin service books, a censer, sanctus bell, box for the holy oils, statues, lights and many other items. Upon Queen Elizabeth's accession in 1558 the whole process was reversed once more and the accounts for 1559 show expenses in purchasing English prayer books, taking down statues, digging out the stone altars once more and, perhaps saddest of all, an expenditure of 5d in taking down and destroying the lovely rood screen which had survived all the previous changes, and which had been built by the parish with such care and at such expense less than a century before. It was no doubt the fact that so many of the screens and benches had been paid for by the parishioners that led several parishes throughout the region, and particularly in Somerset, to disobey the various government edicts and retain their rood screens and their carved benches.

During the succeeding centuries, parish churches were subject to many further alterations in response to changing religious fashions, the need to accommodate increased populations, or because of restoration and re-building, and part of the fascination of looking at the interiors of many churches in the region consists of seeing the way in which remnants and evidences survive of many former religious fashions and traditions, often superimposed one upon the other. The seventeenth century saw the re-introduction of screens into many churches, and the installation of pulpits, box-pews and galleries. Magnificent examples of complete seventeenth-century interiors fitted into a medieval church are to be seen at Croscombe in Somerset.

There are many surviving examples of eighteenth-century interiors, with box-pews, 'three-decker' pulpits consisting of pulpit, reading desk and a stall for the parish clerk in descending order, and the galleries for the accommodation of the poor and those who could not afford to rent a seat in the body of the church. Excellent eighteenth-century interiors are to be seen for example at Mildenhall and Old Dilton in Wiltshire, at Cameley and Holcombe in Somerset, or in Dorset at Chalbury, Winterborne Tomson or St George's, Portland. Nineteenth-century restorations and rebuildings of churches abound throughout the region, especially in those parishes where there was a resident squire or some other wealthy benefactor to bear the expense of the work. In Wiltshire, for example, in the main period of church building and restoring in the half century between 1837 and 1887, 32 churches were enlarged, 98 were restored, 51 rebuilt and 45 completely new churches erected. In Dorset during the period 1840–76 there were 233 parish churches, of which 158 had more than £500 spent upon them, and many had several thousand pounds spent in lavish restoration or rebuilding.

One example out of many of individual generosity and zeal for church building and restoration was Mary Caroline, Marchioness of Ailesbury, who lived at Tottenham House in Savernake Forest from 1837 to 1879 and was largely responsible for the rebuilding or restoration of nearly all the parish churches in that part of Wiltshire, as well as for the construction of four new churches. Several parish churches in various parts of the region still retain the separate and generally very ornate pew for the squire or patron. A magnificent example of this is the Pouletts' large family pew, which is really more like a drawing-room, attached to the church at Hinton St George. Other examples can be seen at Crowcombe in Somerset, Compton Bassett and Lydiard Tregoze in Wiltshire and at Iwerne Courtney and Trent in Dorset. The interior arrangement of such churches, with the lord of the manor and his family in their separate pew, the farmers and well-to-do inhabitants of the parish in their own rented pews in the nave, and the labourers and the poor on the benches in the gallery, mirrored precisely the social gradations and disparity of rural society throughout the period 1500–1900.

An important feature of church services in the country parish churches throughout much of the period was the fact that the music was supplied by a group of village musicians, generally accommodated in the west gallery and performing upon a variety of different stringed and wind instruments. John Aubrey described the village musicians and singers at Bishops Cannings during the early seventeenth century who were sufficiently skilled to be able to entertain James I and his Queen with a musical festival as they passed through the village. This parish would, in Aubrey's words, have 'challenged all England for musique, singing and footeball play'. During the eighteenth and early nineteenth centuries most village churches had their musicians, frequently playing both in church and for village dances and other entertainments, the same tunes played in different time often serving for both sorts of occasions. Such bands with their motley collection of instruments—clarinets, flutes, violins, viols, serpents, etc.—did not accord with the tastes or the desire for 'seemliness' of many parsons during the nineteenth century, and were gradually replaced, often successively by barrel organ, harmonium and finally by an organ. For example, at Purton in Wiltshire where the music for the services had been supplied by flutes and viols played by village musicians seated in the west gallery, an organ was acquired in 1851 whereupon all the musicians resigned and left the church. During an episcopal visitation of Dorset in 1750 the bishop noted that at Melbury there was 'an unhappy difference' between the rector and the village musicians 'about singing of psalms with various instruments'. The bishop managed to compose the quarrel by forbidding the use of the instruments, 'and both parties promised to live in better concord for the future'. This incident is particularly interesting because of the fact that Thomas Hardy's mother came from Melbury Osmund and that Hardy, whose father and grandfather had both been church musicians, based his story of *Under the Greenwood Tree* upon just such a quarrel between the incumbent and his musicians, and set it in that part of Dorset. An example of the way in which the accompaniment of the church services by village musicians was replaced by an organ is to be seen in the churchwardens' accounts of Crewkerne in Somerset. Throughout the eighteenth and early nineteenth centuries there are occasional references in the accounts to small sums being spent on the upkeep of the musical instruments of the church. For example, in 1782 a 'Tennors Violin for the use of the church' was purchased at the cost of £1 11s 6d; and in 1785 the bassoon was repaired for 3s 6d, and a new box of reeds bought for £3. In 1792 a bass viol was bought for £7 7s 0d and in 1797 the churchwardens paid 4s for 'hairing two bows'. There were also occasional references to the singers and to 'the singers' gallery'. These irregular and comparatively small expenses for the provision of music in the church continued until 1823. In that year the curate at Crewkerne, the Rev. Dr Robert Hoadley Ashe, presented the church with the gift of a new, London-made organ. The musicians' services were evidently dispensed with immediately, but the churchwardens were to find that the new method of providing music was far more expensive than the old. Soon afterwards the accounts show an expenditure of £25 per annum paid to Mrs Budden, the organist, for her salary and 'To Richard Marsh for attending and blowing the Organ at £2 0s 0d for the year'. Mrs Budden also had to be provided with printed sheet-music at a cost of £1 8s 6d. In 1826 she was succeeded as organist by John Summerhays, whose annual salary was £30 'for playing the Organ and teaching the children to sing', and he also demanded music books at a cost of £2 8s 0d. By his generous and no doubt kindly-meant gift Dr Ashe had vastly increased the Crewkerne churchwardens' expenditure on the music of the church; we can only hope that they felt the results were worth it. Similar details of the disappearance of the village musicians and their eventual replacement by an organ are to be found in a great many church-wardens' accounts from churches throughout the region.

Elizabethan legislation made attendance at the services of the parish church compulsory, and churchwardens' presentments or reports to the bishop during the early seventeenth century commonly list persons who had failed to attend church, as well as those said to be guilty of other, more serious, offences. During the seventeenth century various non-conformist denominations began to appear in the towns and villages of the region, and to provide an alternative religious service to that offered in the parish church. Typical of many places in the region was the religious history of the little village of Ryme Intrinseca in north Dorset during that period. Early in the century there was already a strong tradition of Puritanism in the place, and it was this which led a wealthy French protestant refugee, Michael Blanchard, to settle there in the 1620s. Puritan feeling was fostered during the 1630s when the rector deserted the parish and went off to be the resident chaplain to the Earl of Peterborough, leaving the parishioners to the care of a number of itinerant preachers. During the next few years many parishioners left the parish church and set up their own dissenting meeting-house, and during the Civil War and Common-wealth Ryme was fiercely puritan and Parliamentarian in its sympathy in spite of—or perhaps because of—the fact that the whole village belonged to the Duchy of Cornwall. After the Restoration the newly installed rector, John Elford, even feared for his life, so hostile were his parishioners. It was no doubt the reputation of Ryme Intrinseca which led George Fox to visit it and preach there in 1668, and soon afterwards it was numbered among the strongest of the Quaker congregations in the county, with its own meeting-house and burial ground. A similar pattern and vigorous growth of dissenting bodies is to be seen during the seventeenth century in many other parishes in West Dorset and South Somerset, an area from which the Duke of Monmouth drew some of his strongest support in 1685.

NONCONFORMITY

In the cloth-working areas of Somerset and Wiltshire, Protestant non-conformity also grew rapidly during the late seventeenth century, and groups of Baptists, Quakers and Congregationalists were to be found in many country parishes. For example, at Southwick near Trowbridge there were said to be 340 non-conformists in the parish in 1676 and only 100 conformists; and in 1670 the Bishop of Salisbury complained of the number of non-conformists in the Warminster district, and about 'divers great and outrageous meetings'. Throughout the region, in Somerset, Dorset and Wiltshire, the strength of early non-conformity can be seen very clearly from the large number of surviving early meeting-houses, which are still a prominent feature of many towns and villages.

This growth of nonconformity continued through the eighteenth century, especially after the preaching of John Wesley and the early Methodists, although, because of the number of other nonconformist churches in the region, it was from these that many of the early converts to Methodism were drawn. In many parts of the region the first Methodist preachers attracted ferocious opposition, but this rapidly died away, and during the nineteenth century the number of Methodist chapels increased dramatically, so that whereas for example in 1800 there were only 13 Methodist chapels in the whole of Wiltshire, by 1900 there were more than 250. The result of this rapid growth in the number of nonconformist churches was that by the middle of the nineteenth century many rural communities possessed three or four or even more chapels of different denominations, in addition to the parish church. The existence of such a large number of nonconformist churches in addition to the Church of England has had an incalculable effect upon both the religious and social life of the region. In the early provision and encouragement of education, charities, friendly societies, the temperance movement and of various recreations and social diversions, as well as in their more obvious religious ministrations and missionary activities, this multitude of different churches has had an immense impact upon all classes of society in the region. The nineteenth-century directories with their lists of the numerous nonconformist chapels and meeting houses in all the towns and villages show the large numbers of different denominations which were often to be found even in small villages; and the Census of Places of Religious Worship which was conducted in 1851 makes this even more apparent. To take only one example, the North Somerset village of Chew Magna in 1851 had a population of 2,124 people, and for any one of these who wished to attend religious worship there was a choice of seven different establishments—two Church of England churches, a Wesleyan Methodist chapel, a Wesleyan Reform chapel, a meeting-house of the Society of Friends, a Baptist chapel and a preaching-room of the Brethren. All except the last of these churches ran a Sunday school and provided some general education in addition to their religious services, and all were active in charitable and benevolent work.

Besides the churches, other organisations and individuals were also active in charitable works. Notable among the many individuals in the region who were concerned with alleviating the lot of the less fortunate members of society were the two remarkable sisters Hannah and Martha More, who did so much for benevolent causes and for education in the western part of the Mendips and Cheddar during the early nineteenth century. The nineteenth century also saw a tremendous expansion of friendly societies in the region, whose concern was to help their members during periods of illness or misfortune. The figures for the number of such societies founded during the first half of the century are an impressive witness to the strength of this movement for self-help, which did so much to mitigate the worst effects of the harsh economic conditions of the time for those who could afford the small weekly subscriptions. In 1796 the number of societies enrolled with the Registrar of Friendly Societies was:

Somerset 114; Wiltshire 19; Dorset 12.

From then until 1855 the numbers enrolled increased very rapidly as follows: Somerset 664; Wiltshire 292; Dorset 167.

The Friendly Societies did an immense amount of good in helping their members to survive temporary periods of poverty, illness or unemployment. Their annual celebrations or 'Club Walks' around the village to the church or chapel, with coloured ribbons and staffs bearing the emblem of the Society and accompanied by the village band, was also an important social occasion in rural life. Many villages had more than one Friendly Society. Wrington in Avon, for example, had a Female Friendly Society established in 1797 and a Men's Friendly Society established in 1822; both survived until well into the twentieth century. On the island of Portland there were six societies—the United Friends founded in the eighteenth century, the Union Society founded in 1801, the Friendly Society founded in 1808, the Brotherly Society founded in 1817, the New Brotherly Society founded in 1821 and the Unanimous Society founded in 1834.

During the sixteenth and seventeenth centuries, before the great growth of non-conformity, social life and charitable activity in the country parishes was dominated by the parish church. Many parishes throughout the region had church houses in which parish meetings and social gatherings were held, and such church houses survive in many villages though not all are still used for their original purpose. Moreover, regular events, such as the rogation-tide procession around the parish bounds, the Easter and Whit-

Monday festivities as well as the Christmas celebrations, were essentially connected with the church, and it is no coincidence that so often the annual fairs were held at the same time as the patronal festival of the parish church. The churches themselves were often used for parish and manorial assemblies, and for the storage of manorial court rolls and other important documents, as well as for schools. Evidences of the former school-rooms survive in several churches, for example at Old Dilton in Wiltshire and at North Cadbury in Somerset, and there is abundant documentary evidence for schools being held in many other churches. The parish churches and churchyards also provided space for recreation. For example, at Stour Provost in Dorset there was an open space beside the church which was described in the seventeenth century as the place 'wherein the parishioners use of custome their playe and pastyme'; and at Up Cerne in Dorset there was an area between the church and the manor house where, according to the seventeenth-century manorial customs, all parishioners were to be allowed 'free liberty to use any lawful recreation as bowling etc. in ye bowling greene without lett or contradiction of the Lord'. At many places, particularly in South Somerset and North Dorset, the game of fives was played in the churchyard in the angle between the tower and the west end of the nave. For example, at Martock in Somerset the evidence of the former fives court is still very clear in the wall of the church, and at Williton in the same county in 1633 two men were bound over by the justices for playing fives in the churchyard:

there hath been of late an idle game used by tossinge of a ball against the Chapple walle of Williton in a narrow place there betwixt two glasse windowes whereby the same windowes were often much torren and defaced to the greate dislike of the inhabitants, especially of those whose seats were next adjoyuinge by reason of the drifte in foul weathers, and also of the often greater charges in amendinge the same . . . .

Likewise at Fordington in Dorset in 1631 the churchwardens reported eight people to the Dean of Salisbury 'for that they have played at a game with a Ball called Fives in the churchyard and thereby have broken the glasse of one of the windowes of the church the reparacion whereof is unto the value of 5s.' In Wiltshire during the seventeenth century there are references to various sports including tennis, cudgels, fives, bowls, stool-ball and bull-baiting, and at Newton Tony cockfighting was said to have taken place in the church itself. The vicar of Alton Pancras in Dorset was reported by his churchwardens in 1608 because he went regularly to nearby Cheselborne 'to footeball upon the sabbothe day'. John Aubrey wrote of a similar kind of game which he called 'Stobbal-play', and which was played in north Wiltshire and the adjoining parts of Gloucestershire and Somerset. 'They smite a ball, stuffed very hard with quills and covered with soale leather, with a staffe, commonly made of withy, about 3 (feet) and a halfe long. Colerne-down is the place so famous and so frequented for stobbal-playing'.

Any outside source of entertainment was regarded with suspicion, as is seen in the chorus of shocked protest which greeted a company of puppet-players who travelled through the strongly puritan area of West Dorset in the autumn of 1630. They were turned out of Dorchester, then under the powerful influence of John White, the saintly vicar of Holy Trinity, and in September 1630 reached Beaminster, another staunchly puritan town which was to be burnt by the royalist troops during the Civil War. The townsfolk of Beaminster were genuinely shocked by the puppet players, '. . . certaine blasphemous shewes and sights which they exercise by way of puppet playinge,' and they complained to the Quarter Sessions that the company

doe exercise their feats not only in the day tyme but also late in the night to the great disturbance of the Townsmen there, and the grievance of divers of the Inhabitants who cannot keepe theire Children and Servants in their houses by reason that they frequent the said shewes and sights late in the night in a disorderly manner.

The puppet-players were duly ordered by the justices to leave the county and not to return. It says a great deal for the dullness of the everyday routine of life in Beaminster that their arrival could cause such havoc in the discipline of children and servants.

ALEHOUSES

As was shown in Chapter 4, there was during the whole of the period 1500–1900 an amazing amount of drunkenness. Until the late eighteenth century when the maintenance of the poor became such an overwhelming problem, by far the commonest entries in the records both of Quarter Sessions and of individual justices are concerned with unlicensed tippling houses, excessive drinking, drunkenness, unlawful gaming and other connected offences; and during the nineteenth century the amount of time and energy devoted by the churches to the Band of Hope and other temperance movements is, in itself, some evidence of the scale of the problem at that time. Examples of concern over excessive drinking during the first part of the period are legion. For example, in 1617 the Dorset justices received a complaint about a tippling-house kept by Thomas Jermyn on the common at Upwey near Weymouth, where there was said to be continual drunkenness, and many men had regularly to be carried away drunk; others were said to have been so drunk that they had fallen into a nearby pond, and the parson was reported to be there very frequently, and was 'many times so drunk that he had to be carried home and could not read divine service on the sabboth day in the morning as he should'. In 1612 the inhabitants of Calne in Wiltshire petitioned the justices to reduce the number of alehouses because of the excessive number and the rivalry which existed between them over which could brew the strongest ale,

. . . thither do resorte all the greate drinkers both of the Town and Countrie to spend theyre tyme in idleness and theyere monie in excessive drinkinge, being partly drunke and halfe mad no officer can well judge whether they be drunk yea or no and therefor cannot punish them according to the law, and all men for the most part love these Cupp companions so well that no man will take upon him to be sworne witness against any drunkard.

In 1646 a petition was presented to the Wiltshire justices signed by two ministers, three churchwardens and 23 others, alleging that there were too many alehouses in Pewsey and that 'our children, servants and pore labourers are often by them drawne into theyse houses to spend theyr moneys and time to our great prejudice in neglectinge our husbandry and other occasions . . .' Earlier, in 1610, an alehousekeeper from Lacock had been reported 'who for his owne gayne and advantage did keep maintayne and suffer to be used in his house unlawful games, that is to saye tables, cards and shuffleboard, and also drunckeness and other misdemeanors to the great disturbance of his neighbours against the peace . . .' In Somerset in 1631 it was complained that there were too many alehouses in Keynsham, Chew Magna, Chewton Mendip, Pensford and district and similar complaints were received from the areas around Ilchester, Wells and Glastonbury. Some inns and alehouses were of course very necessary for travellers, such as the alehouse at Martock in 1627 which was described as

a convenient clenly house for the parishioners sometimes to refresh themselves in, being so far from the parish church that often times on the Sabbath day and other hollydaies they cannot go home and come again to church the same day; and for that the women of the parish when they bring theire young children to be christened do often stay there to warm theire babes, coming sometimes a mile, sometimes two, from home in the cold.

The puritan clergy and parishioners fought a long and eventually successful battle against church ales, particularly in Somerset where they had long been very popular as convivial gatherings held to raise money for the church, and were important social functions for rural communities. Apart from the pressure of clergy and the church hierarchy to suppress the church ales, puritan gentry could also bring about their ending, as for example the fervent puritan Sir Francis Hastings who by his will of *circa* 1596 left various sums of money to the churches at North Cadbury, South Cadbury, Maperton and Holton in South Somerset 'upon condition that they never use againe theyr churchales, to the prophaning of the Lorde's Sabaothe, the abusing of his creatures in dronkennes and ryott, and the corrupting of their youth by trayning them up in gaminge and lascivious wantonnes and sundry other disorders . . .'

Such popular public holidays and revels were not always easily suppressed however, and many parishes continued to celebrate their patronal festivals with secular revelry throughout the period. At Batheaston, for example, the patronal feast of St John the Baptist on 24 June was the occasion of great celebration in the village in spite of attempts to suppress it. In 1776 the magistrates of the Bath forum division put an announcement in the *Bath Chronicle* that all such revels in the locality were to be suppressed on the grounds that

the Custom of Keeping Revels in the several parishes within the division aforesaid, hath occasioned idleness, drunkenness, riots, gaming and all manner of vice, immorality, and profaness amongst the lowest class of people, to the evil example of others, and the great disturbance, damage and terror of the well disposed, as well as tending greatly to the increase of the poor. . . .

SUPERSTITIONS AND FOLK CUSTOMS

In the small, tightly-knit rural communities of the region superstitious beliefs and practices were common and the surviving records contain many references to superstitions, magic, witches and accusations of witchcraft. It is not possible to examine this large subject in detail here, but the sort of difficulty which could, for example, face a person who had some skill in treating sick cattle, or even sick people, is shown in the case of Joan Guppy of South Perrott in Somerset who was accused of witchcraft in the early seventeenth century and was obliged to provide herself with a certificate signed by her neighbours stating that she was not a witch, but that she 'hath donne good to many people as well in Curinge of dyvers people of wounds and such like things and in drenchinge of cattell and such like Exercises and hath always lyved of good name and fame without any spott or touch of Sorcerye or witchcraft'. Many old women in a similar predicament were not so fortunate in their neighbours. For example, at Rode on the borders of Wiltshire and Somerset a large party of men arrived in July 1694 and proceeded to seize several old women who were suspected of witchcraft and to throw them into the river, in the belief that witches would not sink. The sort of power which could be exercised in a rural community by a person possessed of a reputation for supernatural powers is seen in the case of Thomas Tyher of Charminster in Dorset who was accused by the churchwardens there in 1616 of

using witchcraft and performing publiclie physicke by unlawful means contrarie unto authorite. Wee present the said Tyher for giving purgations unto those that be with child and unmarried and harlots and such like. Wee present him also for saying that Joanne Blick of Charminster had seven devilles in her and for undertaking to cast them out of her.

The presentment goes on to describe Tyher's relations with various women in the parish and his hold over some of the men in an excess of detail too horrific to bear repeating here, but which nonetheless illustrate very powerfully the superstitious awe and regard in which he was held.

It was not only the unlearned who were affected by superstitious beliefs. William Locke, the rector of Askerswell in Dorset from 1674–86, cast the horoscopes of his two children and copied the details into the parish register; and there are many other similar examples. Nor were superstitious beliefs and practices confined to the early part of our period, for many superstitions survived strongly in rural parishes throughout the nineteenth century. In 1816, some 50 members of the Methodist society on the island of Portland were expelled from the church for refusing to renounce their belief in witchcraft; and in the 1860s the vicar of Blagdon in Somerset complained that his parishioners always resorted to a 'wise woman' or 'white witch' for the cure of their sick cattle.

An unamiable rural custom which continued in many parts of the region was that of publicly shaming and ridiculing persons or couples who had offended against accepted standards by a 'Skimmington'. Dummy figures representing the persons involved were paraded around the village to the accompaniment of makeshift musical instruments, and the parade generally concluded at the house of the victim, possibly with the burning of the effigy. Occasionally such processions were continued for two or three nights. There are many references and descriptions of such 'Skimmingtons' including the most famous of all, the fictional account in Hardy's *Mayor of Casterbridge*. In all its details, this resembles very closely other and much earlier accounts of similar processions. For example at Calne in Wiltshire in 1618 where Thomas Wells had allowed himself to be continually nagged and beaten by his wife a large procession was formed one night with effigies of the couple dressed in various fancy trimmings and mounted on a horse facing the tail. The company included a band consisting of drums, guns, pots and pans, pipes, horns, cow-bells and other bells. Having arrived late at night at the house of the offending couple, they threw stones at the windows, and finally burnt the effigies. In some parishes, such processions were not unknown in the early twentieth century.

One aspect of rural life which has almost totally disappeared, except in a very few places, was the regular round of folk-customs and ceremonies which every year marked the passage of the seasons. Each village often had its own particular series of customs, and many of them also possessed their own folksongs which accompanied the festivities.

Many of these ceremonies and folk-customs were of great antiquity, their origins and original purpose long since lost. For example, the ceremony of 'clipping the church' occurred in several places, and consisted of dancing round the church, generally by the men of the village holding hands to make a large ring encircling the church. The dance ended with a great shout and sometimes also with a rush to a particular spot, all said to be designed to frighten the devil away for a year. Such dances occurred for example at Painswick in Gloucestershire, at Rode on the borders of Wiltshire and Somerset and at Langford Budville in west Somerset. Undoubtedly the origin of the ceremony is very ancient and it is probably a survival from some pre-Christian festival which was incorporated by the church into its own calendar.

The festivities and ceremonies which everywhere marked the Christmas season, the decorations, carolling and wassailling, mummers' plays and the Boxing Day customs were also of great antiquity, and these have survived longer and in greater numbers than most other seasonal rural customs. The texts of some of the mummers' plays have been recorded, and a few continue as at Marshfield in Gloucestershire and Longparish in Hampshire. Other seasons also had their own particular observances and customs: Shrove Tuesday was marked by 'shroving' customs and rough games. At Corfe Castle, for example, the closely-knit society of quarrymen who possessed their own jealously-guarded ancient series of rules for working the Purbeck quarries, accepted new apprentices into their company on Shrove Tuesday, after a period of seven years probation. Before being made free to work the quarries on his own, the new member had to pay to the wardens of the company 6s 8d, a penny loaf and beer for the other members of the company. The last man of the company to be married in any year had also to provide a football, which was then used for a rough game all along the road to the little port of Ower, demonstrating the company's right of passage for their stone. Again, this was a very ancient custom, and one which illustrates the mixture of serious purpose and recreation which characterised many of these observances. Another custom which was almost universal and which had a similar practical purpose was the beating of the parish bounds at Rogationtide; the processions were frequently a mixture of horse-play, feasting, drinking and merriment, much of it designed to impress the various points of the parish boundary upon the memory of the participants. This was very important in areas like the chalklands where there were few hedges to mark the divisions between parishes or between the areas of common grazing belonging to neighbouring manors. The practice died out in most places as enclosures created permanent hedges to mark the boundaries. For example, as early as 1608 the churchwardens at Long Burton, Netherbury, Mapperton and other places in Dorset reported that they had ceased their Rogationtide processions around the parish because 'The enclosures have made the bounds so certain wee held itt fitt to be omitted', and also 'because of the multitude of enclosures wee cannot goe.' Refreshment for those who walked the parish bounds were according to custom provided by householders and farmers along the route, and also by the church-wardens. For example, the churchwardens at Wilton in Somerset paid the large sum of £1 13s 4½d for 'meate, drinke, breade and other things at the Perambulation' in 1718. In some large parishes the boundary was so long that two or even three days were required to perambulate the whole of it.

Some places also had Easter Sunday traditions of procession or other ceremonies, many of them dating from long before the Reformation. At Marnhull in north Dorset there was an annual distribution of bread, cheese and beer in the parish church by the parson on Easter Day. As much beer was provided as could be brewed from a bushel of malt, as much 'good white bread not ordinary' as could be made from four bushells of wheat, and 110 lb of 'ordinary cheese' or 100 lb of best cheese. The bread and cheese was cut up into small pieces and together with the beer was brought into the church after Evening Prayer. Whitsuntide and May Day were both particularly important in the calendar of folk-customs and observances. The numerous friendly societies of the west country traditionally held their 'walks' or processions through the towns and villages on Whit-Monday, thus continuing a medieval tradition of the older gilds. The procession generally ended with a church service followed by a meal and games. Other traditional Whitsun pastimes involved the figures of Robin Hood and Little John. Again this was the continuation of an ancient tradition, and the medieval churchwardens' accounts of, for example, Yeovil and elsewhere contain many references to spring-time fund-raising by Robin Hood or 'Robarte Hood'. During the reign of Elizabeth witnesses in a court case at Weymouth described the spring games held in 'divers Towns and villages within the county of Dorset'. These were said to be 'used at the Springe tyme of the yere only of purpose to make sporte and pastyme amonge themselves on Sondaies and other holy daies as also to continewe honest company and mutual society with neighbours.' The practice was said to be to 'elecete and chuse one of the Inhabitants to be Robin Hoode and another Lyttell John, which persons have (always) bin appointed for the Trayneinge and Enstructinge of the youth into divers kinds of activity and vertuous exercises. . . .' At Lyme Regis the Whitsun ceremonies were described in 1609 as 'going forth with a drum, Ancient (i.e. flag-bearer) and flag and Musycall Instruments on Whitsunday morning to fetch in bowes (boughs) and so go to breakfast before morning prayers.'

Wishford in Wiltshire has a well-known custom on 29 May which is held to establish the villagers' right to gather wood in the nearby Grovely Wood. Again, this combines a serious purpose with feasting and merry-making. 'Oakapple Day' on 29 May, which commemorated the escape of Charles II after the battle of Worcester in 1651 by hiding in an oak tree and his restoration in 1660, was a popular festival among rural communities, as was also November the Fifth which commemmorated both the discovery of the Gunpowder Plot in 1605 and the landing of William of Orange in 1688. On these occasions it was usual to ring the church bells, and most churchwardens' accounts contain references to payments for the ringers and to the provision of refreshment for them. At Crewkerne in Somerset it was also the tradition to 'play the engine' on these days, that is to squirt water from the town fire-engine round the market square, a custom which neatly combined rejoicing, horse-play, a holiday spectacle and practice for the town firemen. The churchwardens' accounts regularly contain entries of payments made 'for playing the Engine' as well as for beer for the firemen and for the grease used to grease the Engine and the leather pipes.

Many other places had regular harvest-home festivities, May games, Morris dancing, church revels held on the patronal festival, and other celebrations. All these, and the countless other annual customs, served to provide popular entertainment and recreation, and also to mark the passage of the year and the change of the seasons. The decline and virtual disappearance of the great majority of these occasions for popular merry-making is one of the great changes which has occurred in rural life during the past century and more.

Finally, one aspect of life in the remote rural communities of the region, at a time before easy communications provided regular contact with other areas, is the strength of local speech-patterns and dialect, so that it was difficult even for persons from one part of the region to understand easily the speech of those from another. For travellers from elsewhere, it was even more difficult and many commented upon the problem this presented even in the nineteenth century. Early in the eighteenth century Daniel Defoe, who had travelled all over the country, visited the Yeovil area in Somerset and wrote that the dialect was more difficult to understand than in any other part of England: '. . . 'tis certain that tho' the tongue be all meer natural English, yet those that are but a little acquainted with them, cannot understand one half of what they say'. At Martock, Defoe visited the school and listened to a boy read from the Bible; he described how one sentence was

'I have put off my coat, how shall I put it on, I have washed my feet, how shall I defile them?'
The boy read this, with his eyes, as I say, full on the text.
'Char a doffed my coat, how shall I don't, char a wash'd my veet, how shall I moil'em?'
How the dexterous dunce could form his mouth to express so readily the words, (which stood right printed in the book) in his country jargon, I could not but admire.

7. Power and authority

The main difference between the way in which the life of rural society was controlled and regulated during most of the period 1500–1900, and the situation in the twentieth century, lies in the fact that there were formerly three distinct legal authorities instead of the one all-powerful state system with which we are familiar. A person living in any west-country village during most of the 400 years with which we are concerned would have been subject not only to the laws of the land administered by the King's judges and by the local Justices of the Peace, but was also likely to have had dealings with the local manorial customs or laws administered through the manorial courts, and also with the ecclesiastical law which was enforced by the church courts. Each of these legal systems played an important part in the life of rural society, and it will be convenient to deal with each separately, even though in the minds of contemporaries there was often much confusion between the three authorities and considerable over-lapping of powers, especially since in small communities it was generally upon the same people that the burden of administration and enforcement of the various laws commonly fell. The chief agents in local government were the Justices of the Peace. Like the Lord Lieutenant of each county, they owed their power and position to the Tudor reorganisation of local government, for the Tudor monarchs used as the cornerstone of their system the unpaid work of local gentlemen who were given the ancient title of 'Justice of the Peace'. Local government also depended heavily upon the unpaid work of other officials—churchwardens, overseers of the poor, waywardens, constables and others. Sir Thomas Smith in his account of the English system of government written in 1565 described the justices as

those in whom at this time for the repressing of robbers, thieves, and vaga-bonds, and all other misdemeanors in the Commonwealth, the Prince putteth his special trust, . . . and generally . . . for the good government of the shire the Prince putteth his trust in them.

The county justices met formally four times a year at the Quarter Sessions, and the accounts of the business conducted at the Sessions, which survive for all the counties in the region, are among the most interesting of local records. The justices dealt with all aspects of daily life from crime and its punishment through the endless disputes over poor relief, bastardy, unlawful gaming and drunkenness, to the licensing of alehouses and concern for roads, bridges, charities and taxation. These matters continued to exercise the attention of the justices throughout the whole period, and in addition successive governments heaped fresh loads of business upon them—regulation of wages, oversight of defence arrangements, responsibility for adequate food supplies and markets, and a host of other matters. For example, the Somerset justices meeting at the Quarter Sessions at Wells in January 1627 dealt among other things with the case of various illegitimate and orphan children; a dispute between the various parishes in the Chew valley over their respective responsibility for maintaining the beacon at Dundry hill and for keeping watch and ward there; settled a similar dispute within the hundred of Horethorne; licensed various alehouses; dealt with complaints about rates from Odcombe, Marston Magna and elsewhere; authorised relief to Grace Mogridge of Porlock who had lost all her possessions 'by reason of a greate and terrible innundation of water'; and gave directions for the maintenance of the King's soldiers as they passed through the county. The Quarter Sessions accounts for the eighteenth and nineteenth centuries show the justices concerned with similar problems and playing the same central role in local administration.

The Dorset justices meeting at the Quarter Sessions in 1635 dealt with matters as diverse as the increase in the number of poor people, the effects of a disastrous fire at Bere Regis in 1634, a dispute over the right to glean corn after harvest in the fields of Sherborne, measures to prevent the spread of plague from Blandford, and a complaint that many inhabitants of Beaminster kept 'great fierce and dangerous doggs by meanes whereof ye Constables and other Inhabitants there are fearful to goe abroad in the night tyme to execute theire office and negotiate theire businesse.' The justices also ordered the alehouse-keepers in Sherborne to sell their wares by certain specified measures and not by the cup or jug, and decreed that the price of the best ale should not be more than one penny per quart, and that they should not 'brew their owne beere of extraordinary strength of purpose to vent the greater quantity.'

Individual justices also had considerable powers to try minor cases and to supervise the administration of the parish officers. Under the justices, the day-to-day affairs in each parish were conducted by other unpaid officers. Chief of these were the churchwardens, who had originally been concerned only with church matters, but upon whom the Tudors also heaped a mass of secular duties, ranging from poor relief to pest control. The churchwardens operated through what had been an ecclesiastical unit, the parish, but which, from the sixteenth century onwards, gradually came to replace the tithing as the main unit of local government. The annual accounts of the churchwardens, together with those of the other unpaid parish officers like the overseers of the poor and the waywardens, survive for many parishes in the region, and are a major source of detailed information about the life of individual parishes.

Visible reminders of the power and authority exercised by local justices and parish officers exist in many places. Parish constables' staves or badges of office survive for many parishes in the region, as do also the stocks used to secure minor offenders. Several west-country parishes also retain their parish prisons or lock-ups, known variously as round-houses or blind-houses, where the parish constable could hold anyone apprehended for a breach of the peace or drunkenness, and where a culprit or suspect might be secured until it was possible to bring him before the justices. Such lock-ups are still a prominent feature of several places, such as Castle Cary and Wells in Somerset, Steeple Ashton and Bromham in Wiltshire and Swanage in Dorset. At Swanage the very solidly built lock-up has the following inscription:

Erected for the Prevention of Vice and Immorality by the
Friends of Religion and good Order AD 1803.

Equally important in the life of many people were the manorial courts. The manorial system continued to exercise control over economic life, particularly in the sheep/corn area of the chalklands, which was also the area most dominated by great estates. Each manor had its own customs, often carefully set out in the records of the manorial court and listed in successive manorial surveys; these customs had the force of law within each manor. The manorial customs dealt with land-holding and transfers, rents, fines and services, common rules for cultivation and management of the arable land and for regulation of the grazing-land for the tenants' sheep and cattle, and rights to timber, stone, fuel and other resources. This body of detailed, customary law, enforced in the manorial court, was the essential framework for the lives of farmers throughout much of the region, and in many places continued to be important until well into the nineteenth century. The differences in the customs to be found in various manors was referred to by the surveyor of the manor of Iwerne Courtney in Dorset in 1553; he wrote that

Their customs are not so universall as if a man have experyence of the customs and services of any mannor he shall thereby have perfect knowledge of all the rest, or if he be experte of the customes of any one mannor in any one countie that he shall nede of no further enstruccions for all the residewe of mannors within that countie.

The boundaries of manors and parishes did not always coincide. Some parishes contained more than one manor; some large manors embraced more than one parish; and many manors straddled across parish boundaries. Like the parishes, the manors also had their officers. Chief of these was the steward who generally held the manorial courts, admitted new tenants, received the lord's rents, heard the complaints and reports or 'presentements' of the tenants' representatives, the 'jury' or 'homage', and supervised the whole manor on behalf of the lord. Other manorial officials included the hayward who had oversight of the grazing and mowing lands and impounded stray cattle; the common shepherd or shepherds who, on many manors, looked after all the tenants' sheep and saw that they were folded systematically across the corn-lands so that every man's land got an equal share of the benefit; and the common cowherd who received the milking-cows from their owners each morning and supervised their grazing until they were returned for the evening milking. Detailed accounts of the duties of the common shepherds and cowherds survive from many manors. Under the control of the shepherd and the cowherd the common grazing-land of the manor could be carefully managed and eaten by the sheep and cattle in a prescribed order. The orders which exist for many manors setting out the regular course in which different parts of the commons and fallows were to be grazed in turn are an impressive denial of the idea of uncontrolled grazing which has sometimes been alleged as a failing of the common-field system of agriculture.

The surviving records of the manorial courts are one of the most informative of all sources of local history, and provide details about land-tenure, rents and services, as well as about the topography, farming practices, crops and improvements on the manor, and about the economic and social life of the community. For example, at the manorial court of Ryme Intrinseca in Dorset in 1632, besides the formal business of granting new tenancies, it is recorded that Joan Lyde paid 3s 4d as a 'heriot' or tax to the lord following the death of her husband George Lyde; Maude Wallis, a widow, was fined 1s 0d for 'not repairinge her house according to the order of this court'; Elizabeth Parker was fined 2s 0d because her cattle had been found feeding in the King's highway and had been impounded by the hayward; Robert Husday was fined 1s od because he and his wife and son had 'made a rescue and took away his cowe from the hayward when he was driving him to the pound'; and two other members of the same family, George and Nicholas Husday were fined 11s 2d 'for assaulting Anthony Wood and drawing bloode of him with batts'; while Anthony Wood's wife, Armirell, was fined 9d for 'assaulting Robert Husday and drawing blood of him'. Such records bring us closer than perhaps any others to the heart of the rural communities of the region.

The eighteenth-century records of the manorial court at Pensford and Publow near Bristol show very similar concerns. In 1737 for example, besides the formal business relating to tenancies and to the little market at Pensford where the market-place survives with its lock-up still ready for those who might have over-indulged themselves, although the market itself has long since ceased, tenants were fined for not keeping their houses in repair, for stray cattle, for 'leaving open ye Colepitt Holes on Leigh Down Commons', for obstructing the road, and for making enclosures on the common. Joseph Coward was ordered to 'pull down his House of Office in one months time or to cleanse the same, it being very offensive'; and Cornelius Duckett was ordered to stop 'throwing his Tann soyle [i.e. foul-smelling waste from his tannery] into the street at Woollard, being very offensive in the footroad and in all the neighbourhood'. The same Cornelius Duckett was also ordered to remove his pigsty, since the smell was 'very prejudiciall to the neighbours'. Rural life was far from being the idyllic existence that romantic painting, or even the present-day appearance of some villages, might suggest.

Until 1860 the church courts continued to exercise power over a great variety of different matters which would now be regarded as of purely secular concern. The ecclesiastical law was therefore of great importance in rural life, and few people escaped from some contact with the legal system operated by the church. The Reformation of the sixteenth century made little difference to the church courts, apart from a few minor reforms and the abolition of appeals to Rome, and the church continued to be the sole arbiter in all matters relating to marriage, adultery and all sexual sins, slander and similar trouble-making, non-payment of tithes or other church dues, failure to observe Holy Days, trading on Sundays and the like, and, most important, all matters relating to wills and testamentary disputes. Wills could be proved only in the church courts, and there all cases relating to wills had to be tried. The records of these courts are therefore a most important source of information on rural life. The probate inventories, or lists of the household goods of recently deceased persons, which are such a valuable source of detailed evidence concerning the everyday lives, wealth and possessions of ordinary people, and which survive in large numbers, were made at the behest of the ecclesiastical authorities and were deposited among the records of the church courts. The records of the dealings of the courts with various offenders provide a valuable insight into otherwise hidden aspects of daily life. This can be illustrated by two examples from Charminster in Dorset. In 1616 Thomas Tyher was brought before the church courts and excommunicated for 'using witchcraft and performing publicklie physicke by unlawful meanes'; in 1631 Ursula Green, also of Charminster, was sentenced by the church courts to perform public penance in the parish church during morning service on a Sunday, 'with a white sheete loose about her, her face uncovered and a white rod in her hand of an ell longe'. She was also to make the following public declaration after the second lesson,

I doe before almighty God and you his church and congregation here present acknowledge and confess that I have most grievously offended his heavenly Majestie in committing the wicked and detestable offence of fornication with Christopher Harbyn for which offence I am hartily sorry and doe unfeignedly repent me of the same. And doe desire you here present not only to pray to God for the forgiveness of my offence, but that it may be an example to you all to avoyd the like and I faithfully promise by God's assistance never to offend in the like againe.

Christopher Harbyn apparently escaped with a caution from the church court.

Offenders were brought to the notice of the ecclesiastical authorities by the annual presentments or reports made by the churchwardens of each parish, in which they gave details both of the church building and also of the moral welfare of the parish. Not infrequently the churchwardens also reported upon the doings of the incumbent. These presentments often also contain fasincating and valuable information for the historian of rural society. For example, at Sherborne in 1615 the churchwardens reported a long list of persons who played at Bowls on the sabbath. A presentment made by the churchwardens of Beaminster in 1634 gives something of the flavour and manner in which a country clergyman addressed his flock. All clergy had been ordered to read the declaration about recreations on Sundays, known as the King's Book, a declaration which gave great offence to many puritan clergy and laity. The Beaminster churchwardens reported

Mr Spratt, our curate, was enjoined to read the King's Majesty's book touching the lawful recreations of the people upon Sundays after evening prayer, which book he read accordingly; but having read it, spake of it in this manner; 'Neighbours (said hee) there is noe one commanded to use these recreations as in this booke is here specifyed but these lawes are left to everyone's discretion whether you will use them or not use them, therefore I doe advise you rather to obey God's lawes rather than the lawes of the King,' or words to that purpose.

Similarly at Halstock near Yeovil in 1613 the churchwardens reported

We present that our minister about Easter last said in his sermon that it were better to eate or drinke before we came to ye communion than to think of our breakfast at home. And that it made noe matter whether we received it sitting, standing or kneeling, but that in his opinion it might best be done sitting.

Church records of the eighteenth and early nineteenth centuries also show that the church authorities/courts remained active and continued to exercise their functions as guardians of morals as well as pursuing the formal concerns of the church courts. For example in 1735 an episcopal visitation of Blandford Forum brought to the attention of the church court the fact that 'Catherine Piddle, Prudence Paine and Christian Adam have had bastards,—imprudent creatures that do penance yearly without shame.'

It is clear from any study of the records of the three legal authorities, the justices and parish officers, the manorial officials or the church, that rural life in the region throughout the period 1500–1900 was far from being the peaceful and placid existence which the romantic view of the past sometimes assumes. The little rural communities of the south-west were no more immune from crime, quarrels and strife than were the towns, and from the number of long-drawn-out civil disputes over land, money, wills and other matters which so often vexed rural society throughout the period, it is easy to see why the legal profession has always provided such a sure and popular route to wealth.

But as well as such disputes and legal affairs which affected individuals, there were several occasions during the four centuries under review when the whole of rural society was disturbed by riots or protests of one sort and another, or when large parts of the region erupted into civil disorder. In general, the rural communities of the region were not easily moved to violent protest and, as was shown in Chapter 4, accepted quietly conditions of daily life which, from the stand-point of the twentieth century, would be thought intolerable; nonetheless there were occasions and issues which roused even the normally placid farmers and labourers to active, violent protest. It is interesting to see just what issues did move them to revolt, or alternatively what matters failed to rouse any concerted protest. None of the radical religious changes of the sixteenth century provoked any united protest in the region. Neither the dissolution of the large number of ancient, wealthy and magnificent religious houses, nor the abolition of the chantries, nor the changes in the language and ritual of the services in the parish churches—nor, perhaps most remarkably of all, the destruction and defacing of many of the things of great beauty and splendour within the parish churches, which the parishioners themselves or their forbears had paid for—caused any open civil disorder or disobedience in the region. No doubt there was a vast amount of individual heart-searching, and great uneasiness at some of the things which were done, but there was no open, violent hostility to the changes. Violence and disorder were however caused early in the seventeenth century over a quite different question. This was the disafforestation and enclosure of the large areas which had formed the royal forests of Melksham or Blackmore, Chippenham, Selwood and Braydon in Wiltshire and Gillingham in Dorset. The result of the dis-afforestation of these areas was to deprive many people of the rights to common grazing which they had previously enjoyed within the royal forests, and during the period 1628–31 the riots in Wiltshire and Dorset, together with similar protests in parts of Gloucestershire provoked by the enclosures in the forest of Dean and elsewhere, constituted what was probably the largest single example of popular uprising in the country during the years before the Civil War. As in riots in southern England two centuries later, when the mythical figure of 'Captain Swing' gave a unity to what would otherwise have been only a disorganised mob, so in the seventeenth-century revolts the mysterious imaginary figure of 'Lady Skimmington' was used to provide a focus of leadership which would otherwise have been lacking. As shown in Chapter 6, a 'Skimmington' was a west-country term for a boisterous mock ceremony held to make fun of a husband who allowed himself to be dominated by his wife, or of a wife who was unfaithful to her husband.

The name of 'Lady Skimmington' occurs in the records relating to the revolts against disafforestation in Gloucestershire, Wiltshire and Dorset, and under her supposed leadership the rebels evidently had a strong and capable organisation. For a time they achieved considerable success. At Gillingham in 1628 the rioters threw down the enclosures that had been made in the royal forest and were able, temporarily, to defy the royal troops sent against them. They proclaimed in splendidly independent fashion 'Here we were born, and here we stay!' In the forest of Braydon in north Wiltshire the commoners rose in revolt in 1631, again under the supposed influence of Lady Skimmington, and for a time were successful in throwing down enclosures and returning the land to common use. Near Warminster the authorities found it difficult to obtain local men who were willing to attack a body of rebels who had established themselves on Cley Hill in 1628 in protest against enclosure proposals affecting the forest of Selwood. Eventually the superior strength of the royal forces and the persistence of the legal processes employed against the rebels defeated the riots in all the affected areas, but while they lasted the revolts posed a serious and difficult problem to the government. The former royal forest remained centres of discontent and disaffection up to the outbreak of the Civil War, and the episodes did nothing to endear the King's cause to the ordinary people of the area.

With the military events of the Civil War, in which the west country played an important part, we are not here concerned, but the passing and repassing of rival armies and the disruption, damage and general disorder caused the total dislocation of ordinary life in many parts of the region, and gave rise to the remarkable protest movement by the 'Clubmen'. The accounts for the Earl of Salisbury's estates in the neighbourhood of Cranborne on the borders of Wiltshire and Dorset show the sort of difficulties that ordinary people faced because of the war, even though they were far removed from the actual fighting. The Earl's agent at Cranborne had arranged in 1643 for much of the best furniture to be taken from the house and sent to the Isle of Wight for safe-keeping. His precautions were only just in time, for during the next three years the house at Cranborne was sacked twice, once by the Parliamentary troops and once by the Royalists. In addition, the accounts show incessant demands for the quartering of soldiers, for money, for the provision of horses, men, food-supplies and other commodities. The tenants on the estate were afraid to attend either the local markets or the manorial court because of their fear of the armies or of small bands of soldiers who roamed the countryside. Even more important, they were unable to cultivate their land, sow their seed or reap their crops. In consequence they were unable to pay their rent. Among many pathetic letters from distressed tenants was one from John Curridge of Tarrant Rushton who wrote in 1647

I have had so manie souldiers that I am not able to pay the rent that is past, for I have had one and twentie that have binn sent unto me with tickets (i.e. authorisation for food and lodging) besides manie others. I have payd contribution monie ever since the warres began . . . Besides there was never no gathering for otes, hay or anie thing whatsoever. . . . They eat up my corne that I was enforst to bye my seede. This is the truth and nothing but the truth.

A similar state of affairs is to be seen in estate records from all over the region, and it was the feeling of helpless outrage among the rural communities in parts of Somerset, Wiltshire and Dorset that led to the remarkable rising of the Clubmen in 1645 and 1646. They claimed to be neutral in the struggle between King and Parliament, and were concerned only to protect themselves and their property against the damage caused by both sides. The movement was strongest in the area around Shaftesbury, Gillingham, Mere and Wincanton, where the three counties meet, and where the memory of the struggle against the enclosure of the royal forest was not dead. This was also an area which had been much affected by the continual passage of rival armies. In March 1645, 1,000 countrymen were reported to be assembled in the area to resist attack, and on 25 May 1645 a large number of farmers and countrymen estimated at 4,000, drawn from all three counties, met on the open downland at Gussage Corner and formed a peace-keeping association 'to assist one another in the mutual defence of our liberties and properties against all plunderers and all other unlawful violence.' In June 1645 similar gatherings were held near Castle Cary in Somerset and at Sturminster Newton in Dorset, and petitions were carried to both King and Parliament demanding a peaceful settlement of the conflict. The Clubmen, as they came to be known, were drawn mainly from the yeomen and farmers, from that section of rural society which was suffering most from the effects of the war. The leadership was provided by a few gentlemen and by several of the parish clergy; and their aims were admirably summarised in the slogan on one of their banners:

> *If you offer to plunder or take our cattle,*
> *Be assured we will give you battle.*

During the summer of 1645 there were several minor clashes and engagements between the Clubmen and small forces of both Royalist and Parliamentary troops, but after the defeat of the royal army at Naseby in June it was the Parliamentary army that the Clubmen saw as the greatest threat to their lives and property. But they were no match for the well-armed, disciplined forces of the Parliamentary army. In August 1645 nearly 2,000 Clubmen opposed the Parliamentary army commanded by Cromwell at Shaftesbury; driven from the town they established themselves within the easily-defended earthworks of the Iron Age fort on Hambledon Hill. After an unsuccessful attempt to negotiate with them, Cromwell was able to dislodge them by a very cleverly organised attack from the rear. A dozen of the Clubmen were killed, and some 300 taken prisoner and locked up in the church at Iwerne Courtney (Shroton), where Cromwell himself lectured them, and made them all promise to be well-behaved in the future, before they were released. Cromwell wrote of them, '. . . they are poor silly creatures . . . [and] they promise to be very dutiful for time to come, and will be hanged before they come out again.' The whole episode of the Clubmen, while not materially affecting the course of the Civil War in the region, remains a remarkable example of protest by the ordinary people, and makes clear the sort of pressures which would lead them to concerted, armed protest. Like the risings against the enclosures of the royal forests, and the later rising of 1830, the Clubmen were making an heroic but hopeless gesture in the face of much stronger forces. None of the risings had any hope of real success, but all are of great interest in revealing the deepest feelings and attachments of rural society.

Other occasions on which people from the region were persuaded into armed revolt included the ill-fated royalist rising in Wiltshire in 1655 led by Colonel John Penruddock and, more notably, the Monmouth rebellion in 1685 which remains the most tragic and pathetic of all the incidents of west-country history. Again, the details of these events are not our concern here, but it is worth noting that all the risings so far listed involved the better-off members of the rural communities, those with wealth or property to protect, or with sufficient leisure and education to hold strong politic or religious opinions. For it is remarkable that although conditions for many people in the region worsened considerably during the eighteenth century, that the combined effects of increasing population, enclosures, new agricultural practices, changing patterns of land-tenure and other developments led to a situation in which many people were much worse off and where conditions for a sizeable proportion of the population were appalling, this situation—affecting mainly the lowest classes—did not provoke armed revolt nor any violent protest. Nor did the harsher regulations of the new Poor Law or the grim conditions of the Union workhouses during the nineteenth century spark off any spontaneous or united opposition, although there were several minor, unco-ordinated protests.

Apart from the isolated and somewhat untypical episode of the Tol-puddle Martyrs of 1833-34, the only sustained attempt by the labouring population of the region to change their miserable lot by the use of force occurred in 1830. The ending of the Napoleonic Wars in 1815 and the consequent recession in agriculture had made conditions for labourers even worse than they had been before and during the war. By 1830 the appallingly low wages, bad conditions and incredibly long hours of work stirred even the normally passive labourers of the west of England to join in the widespread rioting, rick-burning and machine-breaking which swept through much of southern England during the autumn of 1830—the notorious 'Captain Swing riots.' The riots were very short-lived, lasting for less than a fortnight in the whole region, and they were suppressed without much difficulty, but nonetheless they served thoroughly to frighten the authorities; it was their alarm on this occasion which, incidentally, led them to over-react so violently against the comparatively innocuous proceedings of the Tolpuddle labourers four years later. The Swing riots spread into Wiltshire from Hampshire and Berkshire on 15 November 1830, with threatening letters addressed to farmers and landowners demanding higher wages and better conditions and warning of the arson and machine-breaking that would follow any refusal. As in other counties, the letters were signed by the mythical 'Captain Swing'. Wages in Wiltshire and Dorset were abysmally low; agricultural labourers were paid less than in any other English county, generally no more than eight shillings a week, and the labourers' demands were limited to asking for a living wage. When the Napoleonic War had ended in 1815 already 15 per cent of the total population of Dorset was receiving parish relief, and conditions for the labourers got steadily worse. William Cobbett, travelling through Wiltshire in 1825, wrote indignantly that he had never seen finer countryside nor had he ever witnessed labouring people who were more miserable. In 1830 the fury of the labourers was directed mainly against the new threshing-machines, which they saw as likely to deprive them of a large part of their traditional winter employment. During the period 15–28 November rioting, rick-burning and the smashing of threshing-machines occurred in many different parts of Wiltshire—in the Wylye valley, at All Cannings near Devizes, around Marlborough and Ramsbury, and in a string of parishes around the edge of Salisbury plain and along the Avon valley. On 23 November when the riots were at their most widespread in Wiltshire, 25 towns and villages were affected in the county; on 25 November a pitched battle occurred at Pyt House near Tisbury between some 400 labourers and a troop of yeomanry which had been sent to disperse them. One labourer was shot dead, several were wounded and 25 arrested. By 28 November the disturbances in Wiltshire were practically over; 97 threshing-machines had been broken, there had been 18 instances of rick-burning, and more than 300 labourers had been arrested. Eventually 399 Wiltshire labourers were brought for trial, of whom 57 were jailed and 152 sentenced to transportation.

The disturbances in Dorset occurred slightly later than those in Wiltshire and Hampshire, and there were two main areas of the county affected—the central chalklands between Dorchester and Wimborne, and the traditionally lawless, unruly region of Cranborne Chase. On 22 November labourers around Bere Regis began assembling to demand a ten-shilling weekly wage, and the movement spread during the next few days to the areas of Wareham and Puddletown, where ricks were burned and threshing-machines broken. At the same time there was widespread rioting in the region between Blandford and Shaftesbury, and at Sixpenny Handley where on 23 November a magistrate reported that 'had we committed for participating in and aiding the burning of machinery we might have committed two-thirds of the labouring population of the district.' Typical of the threatening letters received by landowners in Dorset was one to Mr Castleman whose estates were in the Wimborne area: 'Sunday night your house shall come down to the Ground for you are an inhuman monster and we will dash out your brains. . . . The Hanley Torches have not forgot you.'

Frenzied activity by the county magistrates in Dorset, with great numbers of special constables sworn in, the yeomanry and coastguards employed to help, as well as some concessions and agreements to raise wages, quietened the rioters, and peace was restored by the end of November. Ten threshing-machines had been broken and 12 ricks fired in the county, and in January 1831 62 Dorset prisoners were tried at Dorchester for their part in the disturbances, of whom 15 were jailed and 13 sentenced to transportation for their part in the attempt to gain a living-wage. The few temporary improvements in wages were quickly lost, and the Dorset farm-labourers were soon in as desperate a condition as before.

Somerset was much less affected by the Swing riots, possibly because of the different type of farming practised over much of the county and the preponderance of smaller, pastoral farms; west Dorset with a similar landscape and farming was also little affected. Nonetheless there were some disturbances in Somerset, along the Wiltshire border at Frome and at Banwell. In all 40 labourers were arrested in the county, of whom 13 were eventually jailed and one transported.

By the end of December 1830 the whole region was quiet once more; the labourers had returned to work, and during the next few months were to see the retribution inflicted upon those of their fellows who had been arrested. The remarkable feature of the Swing rising or of the other occasional, isolated instances of violent protest against conditions, is not that they occurred, but that in view of the low wages and atrocious conditions of many farm-labourers in the region there were not far more such occasions, and that the Wessex labourers remained generally so submissive to power and authority.

THE CARE OF THE POOR

The period 1500–1900 was one which saw the problems of poverty and the care of the poor grow to ever more serious proportions, and for the greater part of the period an ever-increasing load of responsibility for dealing with the poor was laid upon the shoulders of the unpaid parish officers. During the middle ages this problem had not been accepted as part of the concern of the state at all, and the duty of relieving the poor and destitute or caring for the friendless sick, fell upon the church. Even after the Reformation, the more conscientious clergy still regarded the relief of the poor as part of their duty. George Herbert, the saintly vicar of Bemerton near Salisbury, could write in 1632 that the model parish priest 'takes care that there be not a beggar or idle person in his parish, but that all be in a competent way of getting their living.' The seventeenth- and eighteenth-century almsboxes which survive in so many churches, and often still bear the legend 'Remember ye Poor', also bear witness to the church's continuing concern for the poor and destitute. But by the sixteenth century the problem had grown too large to be solved purely by voluntary charity, and a whole series of acts were passed which attempted to discriminate between on the one hand the 'sturdy beggars and vagabonds' who were 'whole and mighty in body and able to labour', thought to have increased so greatly in numbers 'by occasion of idleness, mother and root of all vices', and who were to be punished by being 'whipped until his or her body be bloody, . . . and sent forthwith . . . to the parish were he was born'; while on the other hand the genuine poor who could not earn their own living were to be maintained by each parish from the proceeds of a parish rate. All this legislation was summed up in the Poor Law Act of 1601, and from then until the reform of the whole system in 1834 much of the time of parish officers was taken up in dealing with the problems of poverty and many of the surviving parish documents relate to this subject. The accounts of the unpaid officials annually appointed in each parish to act as Overseers of the Poor show the way in which each parish attempted to cope with its own poor, the way in which vagabonds and beggars were punished and sent to their own parishes, the zealous care with which Overseers prevented anyone who might possibly become a charge on the poor-rates from settling in the parish, and the remarkable mixture of compassion and harshness with which they discharged their responsibilities towards the poor and unfortunate within their parishes. The Overseers were in an impossible situation: concerned to keep the rates down within their own parish; fearful of showing too much leniency lest they should encourage paupers to apply for parish relief, yet subject to the oversight of the local justices; anxious to do the right things and to discharge their responsibility fairly, and often displaying also understandable human compassion towards those who were forced to seek relief from them. All these conflicting factors are to be seen in any of the multitude of surviving Overseers' account books. For example one of the Overseers at Chew Magna near Bristol made the following entries in his account book for May 1707:

Concerning John Taylor and my expenses in keeping him from being a parrishioner here	2s	0d
For sending Abigall Cox and her base child to Felton	1s	6d
Gave Margaret Stone in her sickness	2s	6d
Paid for a bed 2 blanketts one covered & a thick covering for Moses Dix and for 2 eles of cloath for a bowlster and ye carrige from Bristol	18s	8d
Pd two men for carrying him to ye church house	1s	6d
Gave Mary Cox for ye Bone setter when her childs arme was broak	4s	0d
Spent at a parish meeting	4s	0d
Pd for a coffing bran ale and Grave for Moses Dix	8s	8d
Gave Sarah Hill towards paying House Rent	2s	0d
Payde for one apron and two shifts for Huppers Child	3s	0d
Payd for two shurts and a pear of shoos for John Vigers son	6s	4d
Gave Tho Kelson to buy spertickels		6d
Payd to Ospitalls	14s	0d
Gave to ye Wid Fooll in her sickness at severall Times	4s	6d
Payd for Caps for Huppers children and neckcloths	2s	11d
Paid for three sacks of Cole for Moses Dix	3s	9d
Pd a man for to fetch ye surgon to Mary Pavior		6d
Pd for ye heyer of ye hos for to cari Mary Pavior		6d
Pd to ye Shurgan in part for Curing of Mary Paviors leg	£1 0s	0d
Gave a poore woman		4d
Gave a poore woman with a certificate for fire		6d
For going to Keynsham on the Account of James Hoopers servant	1s	6d
Gave to two poore women that was like to lay upon us		9d
Pd to Mary Jenkins for tending of Ann Parsons when she had the Small Pox	6s	0d
For carrying a vagabond to Stanton	2s	8d
To a poor woman and 6 children	2s	6d
To a great Bellyed woman to send her towards Wrington	1s	6d

The changes in agriculture and the decline in real wages paid to farm labourers in the Wessex region during the eighteenth and early nineteenth centuries meant that the demands made upon the parish poor-rates increased alarmingly; for labourers and their families the conditions meant that they could hardly hope to live out their lives without at least some temporary recourse to the parish overseers, and for many the parish poorhouse was their inevitable destination as soon as they became too old or too ill to work. The dramatic increase in the number of persons asking for relief and the alarming rise in the parish rates meant that overseers became ever more anxious to pass on paupers to other parishes wherever possible or to save expense in other ways. For example, illigitimate children became a charge upon parish poor relief and overseers went to great lengths to avoid this, either by apprenticing children as early as possible or, better still, by avoiding the problem altogether. Records of the apprenticing of pauper children, often at a very young age and to 'husbandry' or 'housewifery' which meant that they were virtually unpaid servants, survive in great numbers for many parishes, and there are also many instances like the following from Blandford Forum in 1780. Mary Harvey had named John Hardy as the father of her illegitimate child; the overseers therefore arrested John Hardy and by a mixture of bribery and coercion he was persuaded to marry the girl. The overseers' expenses in the matter were as follows:

Licence to marry John Hardy	£2	0s	6d
To John Hardy as a premium	£2	2s	0d
A gold ring		7s	6d
Marriage		7s	6d
Expense at White Hart	£1	15s	0d
To two men guarding John Hardy two night and part of two days		8s	0d

It was obviously cheaper for the overseers to bear the whole expense of the wedding and to pay John Hardy two guineas as a bribe, rather than to support mother and child for some years. Even better was to avoid the situation altogether, and there are countless examples like the following one from Wool in Dorset where the overseers were able to pass the problem on to some other parish. The accounts for 1833 have the following entry:

20 July 1833	Relieved a travelling woman and her two children	1s	0d
22 July 1833	The above woman being in the family way, having refused to leave the parish gave her to leave	2s	0d
	Paid Christopher Brown for conveying her to the next parish	1s	0d

Since each parish was obliged to maintain its own poor, and since each person had a legal place of settlement, there were frequent and often costly disputes at law between parishes about their respective responsibilities, and paupers were obliged to go to their place of settlement in order to obtain relief. The business of deciding where a person's legal place of settlement was had to be done by examination before a justice of the peace, and these 'settlement examinations' together with other records of settlement disputes provide a wealth of detail about the lives of just that class of person who does not normally figure in any other official documents and who has seldom left any other written record. One example out of many must serve to illustrate this. In 1826 Deborah Tucker, a widow of 48 years old, applied to the parish officers at Cerne Abbas for poor relief. They disclaimed responsibility for her maintainance and brought her before a justice of the peace to be examined as to her place of settlement. Her brief life-story which emerged must have been typical of many poor women whose doings seldom appear in the surviving records. She had been born in Cerne Abbas and brought up there, and that was her original place of settlement. Her father had died when she was seven, but she lived with her mother until she was fourteen. She then had a variety of jobs as a household and farm servant at Sherborne, Salisbury, Cerne Abbas and elsewhere, much of the time working out of doors, the sort of life which no doubt explained why she needed parish relief at the age of 48. While working near Wareham in 1797 she had met John Tucker, then in the Royal Marines, and was married. She would have lost her original place of legal settlement and taken that of her husband in Plymouth for some time, and then, when he had got his discharge from the Marines, they both came back to Cerne Abbas where her husband worked as a labourer for several years before his death. Neighbours from Cerne Abbas were produced to testify that John Tucker had been heard to say that he came originally from Frome in Somerset and that was his place of settlement. Although she had never been to Fome in her life, it was there that Deborah Tucker was legally 'settled' and it was the overseers of Frome who had to maintain her. Again the mixture of harshness and compassion in the administration of the Poor Law is evident, for it was ordered by the justices on 16 March 1826 'that Deborah Tucker be conveyed to Frome'; but on the same day the order was suspended on the grounds 'that she can not travel by reason of sickness and infirmity'. Three months later on 7 July 1826 Deborah Tucker was conveyed to Frome, and the overseers of Frome were ordered to pay £18 4s 6d to the parish officers at Cerne Abbas for the cost of moving her and of maintaining her since the original order was made. Deborah Tucker was accordingly forced to end her days among total strangers in the parish poorhouse at Frome. A similar destiny awaited many if not most of the poorer classes in rural society.

In 1834 the whole system of dealing with poverty was radically changed; parishes were grouped together into 'unions', and relief was provided only in the union workhouse, where conditions were intentionally made unattractive in order to discourage applicants for relief. These workhouses were loathed and feared by the poor with a hatred far more fierce and bitter than had been the case with the parish poorhouses: many of the stern, forbidding and solidly-built union workhouses survive as an abiding monument to the nineteenth-century method of dealing with the problem of poverty.

The foregoing chapters have shown that much of the region continued to be dominated by great estates and by the power and influence of the great landowners. The disparity between the rich and poor in rural society, and the extent to which the gap between the classes had widened by the latter part of the nineteenth century, is nowhere better illustrated than by the contrast between the conditions of the farm-labourers, which has been discussed in Chapter 4, and the wealth and possessions of the landed gentry which were revealed by the enquiry into the ownership of land in England made by Parliament in 1872–73, and published as *Return of Owners of Land* in 1874. This enquiry, which was described as a 'new Domesday Book', showed very clearly the extent of the estates and the size of the rent-income of the landowning class at the height of its power and opulence, and before the depression of agriculture in the later nineteenth century. In this survey both Dorset and Wiltshire are shown among the counties with the highest concentration of vast estates of more than 10,000 acres. In both counties no less than 36 per cent of the total area was occupied by such great estates as against a national average of 24 per cent; Hampshire and Somerset were both below the national average for the area occupied by such estates, in Hampshire they accounted for 21 per cent of the total area, and in Somerset 20 per cent. Hampshire, however was among the highest of the English counties in the proportion of its total area occupied by estates of from 1,000 to 10,000 acreages, with a proportion of 38 per cent against the national figure of 29 per cent. The figures for the other counties were Dorset 35 per cent, Somerset 30 per cent and Wiltshire 30 per cent. The enquiry also for the first time revealed publicly the vast possessions of individual landowners in the region. For example, the Marquis of Bath whose seat was at Longleat owned 55,000 acres, of which 20,000 acres were in Wiltshire and 8,000 in Somerset;

the Earl of Pembroke who lived at Wilton House owned 42,244 acres in Wiltshire or some 5 per cent of the whole county. George Wingfield-Digby of Sherborne Castle owned 21,000 acres in Dorset and 5,000 in Somerset; the Earl of Ilchester possessed 16,000 acres in Dorset, 13,000 acres in Somerset and 2,000 acres in Wiltshire. Many other similar examples of vast estates in the region could be quoted, and although many of these estates were benevolent and paternalistic in their attitude to tenants and employees, their continuing existence and great wealth contrasting so markedly with the poverty of many people in rural society remains one of the principal features of rural life in the region between 1500 and 1900.

Select Bibliography

The following bibliography lists some of the more useful modern books and reprints; it does not attempt to be definitive nor does it include the multitude of histories of particular parishes written in recent years, many of which contain much useful information on rural life. Indispensable for any serious study are the volumes which have so far been published of the Victoria County Histories, and of the Royal Commission on Historical Monuments, the Proceedings of the various County Archaeological Societies and the volumes of the County Record Societies, all of which are packed with valuable information, as is also the long series of *Somerset and Dorset Notes and Queries*.

R. ATTHILL: *Old Mendip* (1964)

R. ATTHILL (ed.): *Mendip: A new Study* (1976)

R. ATTHILL: *The Somerset and Dorset Railway* (1967)

J. AUBREY: *Natural History of Wiltshire* (Reprint, 1969)

M. BARLEY: *The English Farmhouse and Cottage* (1958)

M. BERESFORD: *History on the Ground* (1958)

M. BERESFORD: *The Lost Villages of England* (1954)

J. H. BETTEY: *Dorset* (1974)

D. BROMWICH and R. DUNNING: *Victorian and Edwardian Somerset from old photographs* (1977)

D. BURNETT: *Dorset Camera 1855–1914* (1974)

D. BURNETT: *Wiltshire Camera 1835–1914* (1975)

S. H. BURTON (ed.): *A West Country Anthology* (1975)

K. R. CLEW: *The Kennet and Avon Canal* (1968)

P. COWLEY: *The Church Houses* (1971)

J. DAY: *Bristol Brass* (1973)

C. G. DOWN and A. J. WARRINGTON: *The History of the Somerset Coalfield* (1971)

R. DOUCH: *A Handbook of Local History: Dorset* (1961)

R. W. DUNNING (ed.): *Christianity in Somerset* (1976)

H. P. R. FINBERG: *Gloucestershire: The History of the Landscape* (1955)

M. FULLER: *West Country Friendly Societies* (1964)

R. GOOD: *The Old Roads of Dorset* (1966)

J. W. GOUGH: *The Mines of Mendip*, first published 1930, revised edition 1967

C. HADFIELD: *The Canals of Southern England* (1955)

Select Bibliography

C. HADFIELD : *The Canals of South West England* (1967)

M. HAVINDEN (ed.): *Husbandry and Marketing in the South-West 1500–1800* (1973)

E. J. HOBSBAWM and G. RUDÉ : *Captain Swing* (1969)

W. G. HOSKINS : *The Making of the English Landscape* (1955)

W. G. HOSKINS : *Local History in England* (1959). New Edition 1973

W. G. HOSKINS : *Fieldwork in Local History* (1967)

K. HUDSON : *Industrial Archaeology of Southern England* (1965)

K. HUDSON : *The Bath and West: A Bicentenary History* (1976)

B. KERR : *Bound to the Soil: A Social History of Dorset 1750–1918* (1968)

R. LLOYD : *Dorset Elizabethans* (1967)

J. DE L. MANN : *The Cloth Industry of the West of England* (1971)

J. MARLOW : *The Tolpuddle Martyrs* (1971)

W. MARSHALL : *The Rural Economy of the West of England*, first published 1796, reprinted 1970, 2 vols

P. MCGRATH : *The Merchant Venturers of Bristol* (1975)

J. S. MOORE (ed.): *The Goods and Chattells of Our Forefathers (Frampton Cotterell and District Probate Inventories, 1539–1804)* (1976)

K. PONTING : *Churches of Wessex* (1977)

K. PONTING : *The Woollen Industry of South-West England* (1971)

K. PONTING : *Wool and Water: Bradford-on-Avon and the River Frome* (1975)

K. PONTING : *Wiltshire Portraits* (1975)

G. P. R. PULMAN : *The Book of the Axe*, first published 1875, reprint 1969

K. ROGERS : *Wiltshire and Somerset Woollen Mills* (1976)

K. ROGERS : *The Newcomen Engine in the West of England* (1976)

B. SHORT : *A Respectable Society: Bridport 1593–1835* (1976)

B. SMITH : *The Cotswolds* (1976)

B. SMITH and E. RALPH : *A History of Bristol and Gloucestershire* (1972)

B. STEWART : *Where is Saint George?—Pagan Imagery in English Folksong* (1977)

W. E. TATE : *The Parish Chest* (1960)

C. TAYLOR : *The Making of the English Landscape: Dorset* (1970)

J. THIRSK (ed.): *Agrarian History of England and Wales. Vol. IV, 1500–1640* (1967)

M. B. WEINSTOCK: *Old Dorset* (1967)

M. WILLIAMS : *The Draining of the Somerset Levels* (1970)

Notes to the Illustrations

1. *The Site of the former Benedictine Monastery at Cerne Abbas, Dorset*
In 1500 the great monastic foundations dominated much of the west-country, both as landowners and as employers of labour; by 1540 all the monasteries had been abolished. This aerial view shows how completely most of the buildings disappeared, as soon as the lead was stripped from the roofs and the stone taken for other buildings. (Cambridge University Collection: copyright reserved.)

2. *The Cerne Giant*
The blatantly masculine figure, 180 feet long and 167 feet wide, cut in the chalk hillside, dominates the village of Cerne Abbas and the site of the former monastery. On stylistic grounds the Giant is thought to date from the Roman period, but there is no documentary reference to him until the eighteenth century, and only legends to suggest the reasons for his origin and remarkable survival. The earthwork above the Giant's head is the Trendle, where the village maypole is said to have been erected. (Aerial photograph by J. E. Hancock.)

3. *The Green Man*
This figure forms one of the bench-ends in Crowcombe church in west Somerset and dates from 1534. Similar figures are to be found carved in churches throughout the west-country, many of them dating from the end of the Middle Ages. Originally the Green Man represented the pre-Christian god of vegetable fertility, and the survival of so many examples is a tribute to the tenacity of the old beliefs and superstitions, particularly in rural areas. (Photograph: J. H. Bettey.)

4. *The Skimmington Ride, Montacute House*
A plaster-work panel from the Hall at Montacute in south Somerset which was built by Edward Phelips at the end of the sixteenth century. It is a surprising subject with which to decorate the principal room of the house, since it depicts an obviously hen-pecked husband being beaten by his wife and then being paraded around the village on a pole. This west-country method of expressing public disapproval and ridicule survived into the twentieth century; it is described in detail in Thomas Hardy's novel *The Mayor of Casterbridge*. (Photograph: The National Trust.)

Notes to the Illustrations

5. *Part of a map of Hazelbury Bryan, Dorset, 1607*
This detailed and beautifully drawn map was made for the Earl of Northumberland by Ralph Treswell in 1607. It shows a typical clayland manor, with a dispersed pattern of settlement and most of the land enclosed to form small fields, although some open commons survive. The field-names, acreages and land-use are given, and the crosses indicate the quality of the land in each field (National Monuments Record.)

6. *Part of the former common arable fields at Wedhampton, near Devizes, Wiltshire*
The complicated pattern of furlongs and strips is shown in this map which was made in 1784. This system whereby individual tenants' holdings were scattered in various parts of the arable fields was common throughout most of the lighter lands of Hampshire, Dorset and Wiltshire. The Wedhampton fields were enclosed by Act of Parliament in the early nineteenth century. (Wiltshire Record Office.)

7. *Surviving common arable fields on the island of Portland*
The only place in the region where a large area of common arable fields can still be seen is on the island of Portland. The strips survived unenclosed on the island because of the large number of small freehold tenants who successfully blocked all attempts at enclosure, and also because of the potential value of the stone under each strip. (Aerial photograph: J. E. Hancock.)

8. *Plan of the town of Corfe Castle in 1585*
This plan drawn by Ralph Treswell illustrates how the little town was totally dominated by the great castle. Although Corfe Castle was a borough and returned two members to Parliament, had a weekly market, and was an important centre of the Purbeck stone trade, it remained small, and, like many of the market towns of the region, it was in many respects little different from a country village. (Reproduced in J. Hutchins—*History of Dorset*, 3rd Ed., 1861–73.)

9. *Wareham in the late eighteenth century*
The plan shows how easily the whole town was contained within the massive Saxon defences which are still one of its most notable features. (Reproduced in J. Hutchins—*History of Dorset*, 3rd Ed., 1861–73.)

10. *Ashmore on Cranborne Chase*
One of the few settlements on the high chalk downland where water was not normally available, the village is clustered around a circular pond. It stands more than 700 ft above sea level, and dates from the Romano-British period, so that it has probably had a continuous existence for at least 1,600 years. (Photograph: J. H. Bettey.)

11. *Henry Hastings, the seventeenth-century squire of Woodland, Dorset*
Henry Hastings was a younger son of the Earl of Huntingdon, and beside Woodland he also possessed lands at Mappowder and Puddletown. Although his life-style was eccentric, he was a leading figure in Dorset society and an

active justice of the peace. The illustration shows him at the age of eighty-seven in 1638; he died in 1650 aged ninety-nine. (Reproduced in J. Hutchins —*History of Dorset*, 3rd Ed., 1861–73.)

12. *Wiltshire Horn Sheep*

Sheep were the back-bone of the farming of the chalkland area of the region, providing both wool and mutton and, above all, supplying the dung which was essential if the thin chalkland soils were to grow satisfactory crops. The Wiltshire and Dorset horn sheep were long-legged and active, admirably suited to finding a living on the chalk downlands by day and being driven down to be close-folded on the arable land each night. (*Farmer's Weekly.*)

13. *Dorset Horn Sheep*

The modern Dorset Horn sheep are an active and adaptable breed, and retain the traditional attributes of the old horned sheep of the county. These included docility, willingness to be close-folded on arable land, and the ability to produce lambs in October and November ready for the Christmas market. The ewes made excellent mothers and were noted for producing twins. These modern Dorset Horns are standing on the earthworks of the deserted medieval village of Bardolfston near Puddletown. (Photograph: J. H. Bettey.)

14. *Sheep Washing at Bratton, Wiltshire, c. 1900*

In the early summer, before shearing, the sheep had to be washed to remove dirt and grime from the wool, and reminders of this laborious annual chore survive in place-names all over the region. The illustration shows the way in which the fast-flowing chalkland streams were used for the washing and the traditional manner in which it was carried out. (Photograph: Alan Andrew.)

15. *Sheep Shearing, c. 1895*

The very large flocks of sheep which were kept on the chalklands meant that the annual sheep-shearing on most farms was a long and arduous task. Often it was undertaken by contract gangs of highly skilled men who could work very rapidly. The illustration shows a shearing gang from Chitterne in Wiltshire. Note the large number of men employed, the variety of head-gear, and the supply of drink for refreshment. The women rolled and packed the shorn fleeces. (Museum of English Rural Life, Reading.)

16. *Bells for Sheep, Oxen and Horses*

In order to keep track of sheep-flocks on the extensive downland grazing, some of the sheep, often the rams, were made to wear bells. The illustration shows some of the various types of bell that were used in Wiltshire together with their leather fastenings. The large bell on the right was worn by oxen when grazing, and the little bell on the far right was part of a horse harness, since in narrow lanes it was useful for a horse-team to give audible warning of their approach. (Courtesy Ralph Whitlock.)

17. *Water-meadows at Nunton, near Salisbury*

From the early seventeenth century until the agricultural changes of the nineteenth century the floated water-meadows were the most important advance in agricultural technique throughout the whole of the chalkland area.

By encouraging a much earlier growth of grass than would have occurred naturally, and by producing abundant crops of hay, the water-meadows made it possible to keep far larger flocks of sheep and cattle than would otherwise have been possible. In this illustration the channels which conveyed the water over the surface of the meadow can be seen, as well as the ridges which kept the water constantly moving and the drainage ditches by which it was returned to the river. (Museum of English Rural Life, Reading.)

18. *The Title Page of George Boswell's Treatise on Watering Meadows, 1779*
George Boswell lived near Puddletown in Dorset and his book on the construction and operation of water-meadows became one of the best-known guides on the subject. Boswell had long practical experience as a farmer and declared that his book was 'not a Bookseller's job, but the result of several years experience.' (Museum of English Rural Life, Reading.)

19. *Wessex Saddleback Pig*
Pig breeds were not standardised until the nineteenth century, when selective breeding and crosses with various foreign types of pig brought about a vast improvement in English pigs. The Wessex Saddleback became very popular throughout the whole region, and was kept in great numbers especially by dairy-farmers engaged in cheese-making who could use the whey for pig feeding. (*Farmer's Weekly.*)

20. *Ploughing with Oxen on Salisbury Plain, c. 1900*
In some parts of the region the ox continued to be used for ploughing throughout the nineteenth century, although in most places it was gradually replaced by the horse. Until the improvement in horse-breeds during the nineteenth century, however, oxen could provide a much stronger, steadier pull on the plough, and were therefore commonly used, particularly on heavy land. The illustration shows an ox-team working at Bratton on the northern edge of Salisbury plain. (Photograph: Alan Andrew.)

21. *Harvesting Wheat*
Wheat was traditionally cut with a 'bagging hook', which is shown here. This preserved the straw which was valuable for thatching. The wheat was then bound into sheaves and stacked in the 'stooks' or 'shocks' which can be seen in the background, before being carried to the rick. (Hereford City Library.)

22. *Harvest Gang at Work*
Again, a crop of wheat is being cut with 'bagging hooks'. Note the large number of men and boys involved in cutting, binding and stooking; also the earthenware jars of refreshment laid conveniently to hand. This scene was photographed at West Camel in south Somerset early in the twentieth century. (Museum of English Rural Life, Reading.)

23. *Wiltshire Wagon*
Each part of the region had its own distinctive style of wagon, best suited to the terrain and the use to which the vehicle was put. Wagons were not much used by farmers before the eighteenth century, since poor roads and inferior

horses limited their usefulness. John Aubrey records that wagons were little used in Wiltshire before the later seventeenth century, and most farmers relied upon the cart or the pack-horse for transport of their goods. The heavy farm wagon, a masterpiece of the carpenters' and wheelwrights' art, really came into its own in the nineteenth century with the introduction of improved breeds of much stronger horses. (Museum of English Rural Life, Reading.)

24. *Hay Harvest*

Hay was by far the most valuable winter feed for livestock, and for many farmers was the only means of keeping their stock through the winter. The hay harvest was therefore vitally important and, before mechanisation, demanded an enormous labour in cutting, turning, carrying and stacking the crop. The illustration shows a scene at Edington, Wiltshire early in the twentieth century. Note the very large number of people involved, the beginnings of mechanisation with the horse-driven elevator, and the cask of refreshment which was essential for those engaged in such hot, heavy work. (Photograph: Alan Andrew.)

25. *Threshing Scene*

The introduction of steam-power revolutionised some of the traditional farming jobs; none more so than threshing. What had been the work of a whole winter could now be accomplished in a couple of days by the peripatetic gangs which followed the threshing-machine from farm to farm. The illustration shows threshing in progress on Salisbury plain about 1900; the sacks are printed with the words Bratton, Westbury. The figure in the foreground is the rat-catcher with his dog. (Photograph: Alan Andrew.)

26. *Granary*

After the corn was threshed it was traditionally stored in a granary built on 'staddle stones' to prevent rats and mice from gaining entry. Without this precaution vermin could wreak havoc upon stored crops. Edward Lisle, who farmed at Crux Easton in Hampshire during the seventeenth century, wrote that before storing any corn it was essential to have 'got dominion over the mice by store of cats, which a gentleman delighting in husbandry ought to value as much as many do their hounds'. The illustration shows a granary which was formerly on the Longleat estate in Wiltshire, and has now been moved to the Wiltshire College of Agriculture at Lackham. (Photograph: J. H. Bettey.)

27. *Agricultural Labourer's Long Service Certificate*

Farm labourers were often poorly paid and badly housed, notwithstanding the fact that they were required to be the masters of a great number of different and intricate skills. This illustration of a Certificate of Merit presented to George Giles in 1839—a time of very bad conditions and great distress for farm labourers—shows something of the condescending attitude which the gentry and farmers adopted towards their employees. For 30 years' unblemished service on the same farm in Dorset, George Giles was presented with a coat and ten shillings. (Museum of English Rural Life, Reading.)

28. *Farm-house interior at Oare on Exmoor 1849*

The artist, W. W. Wheatley, recorded that he had gone to Oare with a driver and guide; calling at a farmhouse for refreshment, 'the old woman fried some bacon and eggs and placed a wooden trencher on the table, on which she placed the hot Frying pan and its contents, from which the driver and guide helped themselves.' Wheatley has depicted himself in the corner sketching the scene. Note the open fire, the motley collection of utensils, and the large spinning-wheel, a common item in countless farmhouses throughout the west country. (Somerset Archaeological Society.)

29. *Collier's dwelling at Radstock 1846*

This drawing by W. W. Wheatley shows the sort of squalid, one-roomed cabin which could be erected very quickly and cheaply, and which was all that many poor people could afford. Few of such dwellings were solidly constructed and scarcely any have survived unaltered. Some indication of the conditions inside can be gained from the fact recorded by the artist that the hovel had an earth floor and that the height from floor to the eaves was four feet. (Somerset Archaeological Society.)

30. *Farm Labourer and his wife, c. 1900*

The photograph shows Ambrose Matthews and his wife from Bratton in Wiltshire. He is wearing a smock-frock, the traditional working dress of west-country farm labourers, together with corduroy trousers and billycock hat. His wife is wearing the typical working dress of sun-bonnet, a black bodice and skirt, covered by an apron. The smock shown here could be opened in front, which was useful for milking and other general farm work. Carters wore shorter smocks, while for tending sheep on the windswept downlands, shepherds had longer smocks closed in front. Many shepherds also wore a long woollen cloak. Aubrey describes the seventeenth-century Wiltshire shepherds wearing 'a long white cloake with a very deep cape, which comes half-way down their backs, made of the locks of the sheep'. (Photograph: Alan Andrew; information from Mrs J. Morrison.)

31. *The Blacksmith's Shop*

The blacksmith was a very important person in the manorial economy, since until mass-produced implements became available in the nineteenth century, most farm-implements and tools were home-made, and the blacksmith was also the farrier, shoeing the farmer's horses and oxen. This drawing by W. W. Wheatley shows the interior of the blacksmith's shop at Monkton Combe near Bath in 1850. Note the large bellows, the horseshoes and various other tools, and what is apparently the church font being used to hold water for 'drenching' the heated iron. (Somerset Archaeological Society.)

32. *Shawford Mill at Rode, Somerset*

A good example of the way in which milling often continued on the same site over many centuries, although the mill-buildings themselves had occasionally to be rebuilt. In 1516 this site was being used both for grinding corn and for fulling cloth, and it continued to be used as a fulling-mill and later also as a dye-house until the end of the nineteenth century. The traditional water-power was supplemented in the mid-nineteenth century by the installation

of a steam-engine. The present building probably dates from the late
eighteenth or early nineteenth century. (Photograph and information from
K. H. Rogers.)

33. *Hand-loom Weaver at work*

This photograph shows the traditional west-country method of cloth production by hand-loom, and illustrates the process which played such an
important part in the economic life of the region throughout the whole period
with which this book is concerned. The loom shown here was photographed
in 1903 at Palmer and Mackay's factory in Trowbridge, a firm which continued producing cloth until 1963, and the loom is typical of the narrow hand-
looms which were used to produce 'cassimeres' during the first half of the
nineteenth century. Although weaving was the last of the processes in the
manufacture of woollen cloth to which power was applied, power-looms had
been in use since the 1840s and by the 1870s hand-loom weaving, which had
traditionally been carried on in weavers' own homes, had given way to factory
production using power-looms. (Courtesy M. J. Lansdown and the *Wiltshire
Times*.)

34. *Wiltshire Creameries, Chippenham*

The coming of the railways revolutionised dairy farming in the region, since
it enabled liquid milk to be dispatched to the towns instead of having first to
be turned into butter and cheese. The nineteenth century also saw the development of a number of wholesale dairy companies for processing liquid
milk. This photograph shows the Chippenham depot of Wiltshire Creameries
in 1924; note the horse-wagons for collecting milk from the farms and the
De Dion Bouton lorry used for the same purpose. (Courtesy M/s A. Wright.)

35. *Quarrying on the Island of Portland*

The expansion of the stone-quarrying industry on Portland during the
eighteenth century to meet the increasing demand for the high-quality stone
created great problems in getting the stone from the high plateau of the island
down to the piers for shipping. In the absence of machinery, the only way
was to harness horses both in front and behind each large block of stone; a
contemporary description records that the horses behind had to 'act as drawbacks to the carriage and prevent its running with too great a velocity down
the steep; the sagacity and exertions of these poor animals in the arduous
employment, is really astonishing; they squat down on their haunches, and
suffer themselves to be dragged for many yards, struggling with all their
strength against the weight that forces them forwards. . . .' This late
eighteenth-century drawing by S. H. Grimm shows the method used, and
gives something of the atmosphere of the bleak and almost treeless island.
(Photograph: J. H. Bettey.)

36. *Peat-Cutting at Ashcott, Somerset*

The digging of peat for fuel was an important employment in the Somerset
Levels as well as on the Dorset heathland. This photograph of *c.* 1900 shows
the peat-blocks being cut out and set to dry in stacks. Note the great depth of
the peat that is being worked, the characteristic wheelbarrow that was used,
and the ubiquitous small casks for cider. (Photograph: A. A. Moon.)

37. *The Village Square at Montacute, 1848*
This drawing by W. W. Wheatley gives a good indication of the appearance of a west-country village in the mid-nineteenth century. Note the unpaved, muddy road, the gateway to Montacute house on the right, the parish church in the background, with the hill which gives the place its name beyond; in the foreground are a row of shops in what is known as 'The Borough'; the barber's pole projects very prominently from one of the shops. (Somerset Archaeological Society.)

38. *High Street, Marlborough, 1853*
The market-place and main thoroughfare of the town, on the high road from Bristol and Bath to London. Note the carrier's wagon, the fine shop-fronts, the street-lighting and the unhurried atmosphere of the street. The structure in the foreground is a weighbridge. (Photograph: J. H. Bettey.)

39. *Excavating the London to Westbury Railway line at Edington c. 1890*
The railways brought vast changes to rural life, not only because of the greatly increased opportunities for the rapid transport of goods and for travel which they brought, but also because of the employment they created and the gangs of navvies who descended upon hitherto remote rural communities as railway-lines were constructed. Notice here the large number of men employed, and the amount of heavy manual work which is obviously still required in spite of the steam shovel. (Photograph: Alan Andrew.)

40. *Market Day at Yeovil c. 1900*
Yeovil is a good example of that multitude of west-country market towns which were so important in the economic and social life of the surrounding communities during the period 1500–1900. Notice the stalls set up along the street as they had been during the whole of the previous four centuries and more; the agricultural implements and the tools stacked up for sale, the cow being driven through the street, and the gas street-light in the foreground. (Photograph: Yeovil Museum.)

41. *The Village Street and Church House, Chew Magna, 1843*
This drawing by W. W. Wheatley illustrates the two institutions which dominated the social life in rural communities—the alehouse and the church house. The church house which is on the edge of the churchyard at Chew Magna was built early in the sixteenth century and used for parish meetings, church ales and other festivities. Later it became a parish poor-house and a school. Similar buildings existed in most other west-country towns and villages. Note the unpaved, muddy street, and the mounting-block beside the inn sign. (Somerset Archaeological Society.)

42. *Old Dilton Church, near Westbury, Wiltshire*
This charming little church has an almost completely unrestored interior. The building itself is medieval in origin; most of the interior furnishings date from the eighteenth century and preserve the atmosphere of a country church before the changes and restorations of the nineteenth century. There are two galleries, one can be seen at the west end beyond the font, and the other,

which was used as the village school-room, appears on the right of the photograph. Notice the beautifully irregular box pews, the 'three-decker' pulpit surmounted by a sounding-board, and the large clock. (Courtesy of M. J. Lansdown and the *Wiltshire Times*.)

43. *Friendly Society Club Walk, Meare, Somerset*
The west-country friendly societies which were established for the mutual protection and benefit of their members were important institutions in many town and villages. The annual 'walk' through the village with banners and decorated staves, and the feast which followed were highlights of the year. Notice the decorations and the beribboned staves with the MBS emblem for Meare Benefit Society. (Somerset County Library.)

44. *Sunday School Treat at Waterrow near Wiveliscombe, Somerset, 1895*
Sunday schools were important social and educational as well as religious institutions in rural parishes. Until the beginning of free and compulsory schooling in the 1870s, Sunday schools had provided the rudiments of education in reading and writing, as well as religious instruction. The treat or outing was a great annual event, eagerly awaited by the children. The banners bear the messages 'God is Love' and 'Heaven our Home'. (Museum of English Rural Life, Reading.)

45. *Wedding Group at Wiveliscombe, Somerset, 1895*
The wedding of 'Mr Murchant', obviously one between two well-to-do families. Notice the top-hats and bowlers, and the very elaborate costumes of the ladies. The solemnity of their expressions is no doubt as much caused by the need to keep quite still during a long exposure as by the importance of the occasion. (Museum of English Rural Life, Reading.)

46. *Dancing around the Church at Rode, Somerset, Shrove Tuesday night, 1848*
This drawing by W. W. Wheatley shows the ancient, annual ceremony of 'clipping the church' or dancing around it, which survived into the nineteenth century in some parts of the region. The apparent object was to create a magical chain against the power of evil and to drive away the devil. In some places the dance ended with a great shout which had the same purpose. Notice that all the dancers are men, that they completely encircle the church, and that they have what appear to be lighted candles in their hats. (Somerset Archaeological Society.)

47. *The Marshfield Mummers*
Some indication of the sort of traditional folk-plays and entertainments which were once to be found in many places can still be seen at Marshfield, where the ancient mummers' play is still performed on Boxing Day. The makeshift costumes and weapons are an established part of the play which consists of a jumble of legends, but is basically the same theme of the conflict between good and evil that appears on so many parish-church gargoyles, corbels and other carvings. The play serves as a reminder of the wealth of similar local ceremonies that marked the various seasons of the year all over the west country. (English Folk Dance and Song Society.)

48. *Association for the Prevention of Robberies and Thefts,*
    Castle Combe, Wiltshire

In the absence of any well-organised police force, property owners frequently banded together in an effort to protect their own estates and goods. The Castle Combe association dates from the late eighteenth century, and many other similar societies were formed at the same time or earlier, throughout the whole region. (Wiltshire Record Office.)

49. *The Lock-up at Swanage, Dorset*

The lock-up or 'blind house' is a prominent, central feature of many west-country villages and towns. This example from Swanage in Dorset bears the inscription 'Erected For the Prevention of Vice and Immorality By the friends of Religion and good Order A.D. 1803'. (Photography: J. H. Bettey.)

50. *Leaving for the Great War, 1914*

This rather faded photograph nonetheless captures the ending of the old rural England. It shows the young men of Bratton, Edington and Tinhead in Wiltshire, who have volunteered for service in the war, being taken off in the cars of the local gentry, amid scenes of great patriotic enthusiasm. Many of these volunteers were never to return, and those who did came back to a new world of rapid change and upheaval very different from that which they had so gaily left in August 1914. (Photograph: Alan Andrew.)

Index

Note: In this index, entries under the names of counties are based on the boundaries as they existed before local government re-organisation in 1974. Under each county's name will be found, firstly, a list of topics which relate to it as a whole, and secondly, a list of place-names within that county which are mentioned in the text. Where several references are given for any one place, the reader will find that these have been sub-divided into topics under that place-name in the body of the index.

Index